BORN TO
ROAR!

DIANE CORY

🐾 DEVOTIONS FOR KIDS 🐾

Warner Press, Inc.
Warner Press and Warner Press logo are trademarks of Warner Press, Inc.

Born to Roar! Devotions for Kids
Written by Diane Cory

Requests for information should be sent to:
Warner Press, Inc.
2902 Enterprise Drive
Anderson, IN 46013
www.warnerpress.org

Editor: Robin Fogle
Cover: Curtis Corzine
Designer: Karen Muilenburg

ISBN: 9781684341597

Printed in USA

ACKNOWLEDGMENTS

I want to dedicate this book to my grandchildren: Maddison, Blaine, Wesley, and Garrett Cory, as well as to any future grandchildren. I consider each of them young lions who are born to roar and destined to be world changers.

I want to thank my literary agent and friend, Karen Hardin, for her support and encouragement throughout the writing process. I also wish to thank my friend, Kristen Tschida, for the hours she spent editing. I couldn't have finished this writing project without her.

TABLE OF CONTENTS

INTRODUCTION TO THE READER

Hello, Friend!

Welcome to *Born to Roar*. Did you know that God's voice can sound like a roaring lion? The Bible says in Job 37:2 (NIV), *Listen! Listen to the roar of his voice; to the rumbling that comes from his mouth.* This Bible verse means that God's voice is bold and fearless in love. It's a voice speaking for what's right and true.

Some animals may run faster and hunt better than the lion, but what makes the lion fearless and a king among animals is its voice. The roar is one of the main things the lion is known for. Boldness makes the lion stand out among the other animals. Did you know that God wants you to have a bold roar too? He wants kids to have a powerful voice in this world.

What's the first thing you think of when you hear about or see a lion? Is it the lion's strength, power, boldness, or roar that captivates you? A lion is animal royalty. It is a grand, astonishing, outstanding, and wonderful animal in appearance. A lion is so special that it is called "King of the Jungle." It is considered brave and protective. What if you were like a lion when it came to the things of God in this world? What if you were brave in standing up for what's right with no fear? What if you knew how to protect your heart from evil—meaning you wouldn't let anyone or anything steal your heart away from God?

Being lion-like means roaring for God in every area of your life. It's looking daily for ways to be brave in your beliefs. It's being creative, inventive, and original—not going with the flow. Lions are willing to fight when they need to. They don't pick fights, but because they are protective of their food, mates, and territory, they fight when necessary. What is your heart willing to fight for?

Lions are also hunters. Do you know how to hunt through the Bible? Do you know how to seek after God without adult help? This book will teach you how to let your life roar for God and with God. It will help you to be confident in who you are. The world wants to make you conform to its ways. Instead, you can change the world and make it more like heaven. You can roar, letting the world know who Jesus is in you, holding nothing back. God looks forward to spending time with you every day through this book. Come and learn to roar!

PART ONE
GETTIN' READY TO ROAR

A Lion's Terrific Traits

Hi, guys! We're getting ready to lift our heads and roar through life. Part one of this book is about a lion's terrific traits. *Gettin' Ready to Roar* is a place to help prepare you to walk in the traits of a lion. You'll find the *Chew on This* scripture reading is fun. *Under the Tree* is your devotional, and in part one you'll be learning about the traits of a lion. Then, it's on to *My Roar*. *My Roar* is always about doing something with what you discover *Under the Tree*. Last of all, *Pondering Paws* journaling launches you into a world of creative writing (or drawing). You'll love it all. **Let's go!**

LION OR LIONESS?

UNDER THE TREE

If I say "lion," what is the first thing that comes to your mind? If I say "lioness," what do you think of? Which is the guy and which is the girl? A lion is a male and a lioness is a female. But, when we say the word "lion" in general, it can mean a male or female cat. The term lion is also the name for all ages, kinds, and types of cats.

In this book, we talk a lot about lions. Though a girl lion is called a lioness, girls can also be thought of as lions. All the lion talk in this book will include guys and girls. It's like when the Bible talks about sons of God. Sons of God can be boys or girls. The "bride of Christ" can be a guy or a girl. When we use the word "police officer," that can be a girl or guy. An actor can be a girl or guy. A mail carrier can be a girl or guy. So, we are going to let the lion in these lessons be a girl or guy.

Yet, the word "girl" doesn't also mean boy, and the word "boy" doesn't also mean girl. The Bible is very clear—God created boys to be boys and girls to be girls. You came into this world as either a guy or a girl. You are God's guy if you are male. You are God's girl if you are female. Genesis 1:27 tells us that God made one person to be male and another to be female. Boys have their own special roar and so do girls. Each sound is different in how you talk and act, for each has been wonderfully made by our Creator God. So, get ready to roar!

MY ROAR

Read Genesis 1:26–31. Notice how God created guys and how He created girls. What did God say and think after He made us? Thank God for how He made you.

8

PONDERING PAWS

Talk to God about something you are struggling with.
Pray and ask for help and answers. Journal what you are hearing.

LIONS HAVE A VOICE

UNDER THE TREE

God loves for your voice to be heard. He loves to hear you share your heart when you spend time with Him. God has given you something to say. The things you speak are important to Him and others. What you say and do is part of your own roar. It makes you uniquely who you are!

The lion's roar is heard first and in every place the lion travels. So, what you speak is one of the first things people know about you. God made us to be a voice for Him. Our life and voice were created for roaring too, so we gain nothing by keeping quiet.

Whether you are shy or not, learn to roar in your own way (loving, writing, dancing, creating, inventing and serving). If you have a talent or gift, use it; that is part of your roar.

This book will teach you to be humble, but also brave, bold, and confident in who you are. You will learn to roar, making you a strong and powerful person for God. So, get ready to roar!

MY ROAR

In *Pondering Paws* on pg 11, what step did you write that you would take? Take that step and tell someone about it.

PONDERING PAWS

Think about how God might want to use your voice and roar.
What first imprint about yourself do you want to make on those you meet?

LIONS PROTECT TERRITORY

UNDER THE TREE

Why should a lion roar? Lions roar to warn other lions how powerful they are. They roar to tell them to stay away from their pride family. They roar to keep mean lions out of their home territory. The Bible refers to Satan as a lion who is on the prowl. 1 Peter 5:8 (NIV1984) says, B*e self-controlled and alert. Your enemy the devil prowls around like a roaring lion looking for someone to devour.*

Where has the enemy marched into your territory? Has he tried to make you afraid in your bedroom at night? Has he made you feel anxious in your classroom at school? Has he caused you to feel like a failure on your sports team? Has the enemy invaded any of your territory? Then it is time to ROAR! Tell the enemy he cannot have any of the places where you hang out. Those places belong to you and God. The devil has no right to be there. Proverbs 28:1 (NIV) says, T*he wicked flee though no one pursues, but the righteous are as bold as a lion.*

The devil is always pretending to be something powerful and good. He even wants to be a lion. But, true lions take their place and overcome evil with good. Your power over the devil comes from accepting Jesus as Lord and Savior. His cross is where He fought and won over the devil. That's where we win too. Jesus came back to life in three days after He died on the cross. That's when He became like a lion. We can become lions too! Stand your ground and the enemy will flee. The lion with the loudest roar wins. Jesus is the lion of the tribe of Judah! His roar shuts the mouth of the enemy. When you know Him, the devil can't come into your space. So, get ready to roar!

MY ROAR

Warn the enemy to stay out of the places where you go. Use your voice! Speak scripture, and roar the name of Jesus. Just tell the enemy that He must leave in Jesus' name. Keep doing it until he flees.

PONDERING PAWS

Talk to God about your struggles and fears. Ask Him what He wants to say to you today. Listen and write what you hear!

LIONS PICK THE RIGHT FRIENDS

UNDER THE TREE

Lions love to be together and live in family groups called prides. A pride can include up to 40 lions, lionesses, and cubs. That's a big family! Lions don't like hanging out with giraffes, tigers, or other types of animals. They only like to be near other lions. The female lions especially like being around other females. They like having a lot of babysitters for their cubs while they are out hunting, since mama lions are the hunters in the family.

God has also made us to live in families and have friends to hang out with. He wants us to have those we can be with during happy and sad moments. Families and friends are given to help us grow and learn. After all, friends should help each other out. In order to make friends, we have to be a friend. God knows that when we team together, everyone accomplishes so much more.

God does care who you hang out with—friends who are good, helpful, and positive for you. The Bible says in 1 Corinthians 15:33 (NIV), *Do not be misled: "Bad company corrupts good character."* This verse is saying that friends don't need to be just like you, but they do need to be the type of friends that make you better. Friends who love Jesus are the best.
So, get ready to roar!

MY ROAR

Take a good look at your friends.
Ask yourself these questions:
- Do they make me feel happy about who I am?
- Do they want to know God and grow closer to Him or do they just go with whatever?
- Think of your own questions and let your heart give you the answers.

PONDERING PAWS

The right kinds of friends can make you better. Share with God what you need most in a friend. Then, ask God to bring you those types of friends!

LIONS LEAVE TIME FOR REST

UNDER THE TREE

Lions can spend up to 20 hours a day sleeping, yet they still have time to hunt and eat. The lion's instinct and impulse to hunt and eat are huge, yet they find time to rest—at times, for more than half a day! In spite of sleeping 20 hours a day, the lion never goes hungry.

Lions really enjoy their hunting outings! Hunting is like a sport to them. Part of being a responsible lion is feeding the family. The rhythm in the life of a lion is to hunt and rest, hunt and rest.

R-E-S-T equals R-elax, E-njoy (have fun), S-leep, and T-alk to God. Making time for God and rest actually allows us to get more done during the day. Are you setting aside time in your day to rest? Are you so busy with sports, dance, and other activities that you have NO time for fun with friends and family? Does being busy all the time make you anxious and worried? Come and be lion-like! Make time to play and rest! Finding your own quiet corner each day will make you strong as a lion. Roar out of busy-ness and into life's joyfulness. Remember, you're gettin' ready to roar.

MY ROAR

After sticking with the schedule you made in *Pondering Paws* on pg 17 for one week, write again about your experience.

PONDERING PAWS

Create a schedule for your week. Include in that schedule
a time to rest and also to enjoy family and friends.

_____

_____

_____

_____

_____

_____

_____

_____

_____

_____

_____

_____

_____

_____

_____

_____

_____

LIONS SERVE LIONS

UNDER THE TREE

What's on a lion's dinner menu? Antelope, hogs, zebra, rhinos, hippos, mice, birds, and rabbit. They will eat just about anything with meat. Did you know that after lions kill, they rarely eat the entire prey? Instead, they leave those yummy leftovers for other animals to finish off. Their ability to share is the mark of a strong and healthy lion.

Lions have big appetites and crave meat. A large male lion can eat as much as 75 pounds of meat at a single meal. How much is 75 pounds? It's the weight of an 11-year-old girl or boy. Lions, for sure, need a lot of food to keep them a strong and forceful presence in the jungle.

In spite of lions needing to eat a lot of food, they are selfless enough to leave leftovers for other lions. Wow! Little children learn how important it is to share. What about God's big children? What do you have in your time, talents, or allowance that you are willing to share with others? Everyone has something to give someone else. What do you have?

Stop before you eat everything! Stop before you eat the whole candy bar. Stop before you eat the full bag of popcorn, or lick the last bit in the peanut butter jar. Be like a lion and leave something for others. Share what you have and get ready to roar.

MY ROAR

In the middle of your rest, work, and play this week, share or give away something. God sees when we sacrifice for others.

PONDERING PAWS

Journal your thoughts on what it means to you
when you hear the words, "Serve God."

LIONS LOVE TEAMWORK

CHEW ON THIS

As iron sharpens iron, so one person sharpens another.
Proverbs 27:17 (NIV)

UNDER THE TREE

Female felines fancy hunting! The female lions do most of the hunting, while the males guard the family pride. Wow! The female lions do all the grocery shopping! Others care for the young lions while their lioness moms are away from the pride. That is cooperation and teamwork, and it's fun!

God smiles when His kids work together with Jesus toward a common purpose. Together is better and easier. A group of friends can become a great team. One person can be like the lion's paw, fighting through prayer. Another person can be like the lion's legs, running to God's Word to solve problems. Still others are like the lion's eyes, ears, nose, and roar, doing what they see God doing.

We can do a lot for God and others, but we can't do everything alone. We weren't born to be solo Supermen and independent Wonderwomen . There are not enough hours in the day to do everything by ourselves that should be done. Some tasks can be given to others who want to help. The word "team" stands for "Together Everyone Achieves More." Just look for a place where you can jump into a good team, and get ready to roar.

MY ROAR

Follow through. Take a step to sharpen your part on a team. Then record how you felt. Some ideas are: sports teams, family projects, plays, school orchestra, family baking or movie night, art, or board games with friends. Work at helping others on your team feel wanted and needed.

PONDERING PAWS

Have you ever been hurt by being excluded from a team? Make a picture or write about it. Ask God to help your heart heal from that bad experience. Journal how you plan to step out again and be on a team.

_____

_____

_____

_____

_____

_____

_____

_____

_____

_____

_____

_____

_____

_____

_____

_____

_____

_____

_____

LIONS FIGHT RIGHT

UNDER THE TREE

Is fighting ever right? There are ways to fight without using fists or physically attacking others.

Lions fight when they need to protect food, territory, and family. Just as lions fight to defend their food, we must fight to defend our daily bread. Our daily bread is God's Word and all that is right and good in His sight.

So, what do you believe in that you are willing to fight for? Is it speaking up against bullying? What about fighting for prayer in your school? Children can fight for what's right, and they do. Here are stories of children who believed homeless children needed a nice home like them. They were too young to build a house, but they helped those who could build.

- Six-year-old Delilah gathered quarters all summer long, then donated $150 to help build new houses for people in need. It made her so happy to be able to help.

- Eight-year-old Sarah built a butterfly box for a family who was moving into a new house.

- Wyatt and Owen, nine and eight-year-olds, raised "200 buckaroos" selling lemonade. They set up the stand after learning that their church had built 200 houses.

- For J.Z.'s tenth birthday party, he asked his friends to give a donation for building homes. Instead of bringing him a present, they gave money toward building a home for someone in need.[1]

Is there something that feels wrong to you and makes your heart hurt when you hear about it? What can you do? Let's get ready to roar!

MY ROAR

What do you believe in? Ask God to give you something you can do to make a difference. Fight right with your voice or help someone in the area that is important to you.

PONDERING PAWS

What are you willing to fight for? Tell God about it in your journal
through pictures or words. Journal what you did and how you did it.
How did you feel?

_____

_____

_____

_____

_____

_____

_____

_____

_____

_____

_____

_____

_____

_____

_____

_____

_____

_____

A LION'S ROAR IS CREATIVE

UNDER THE TREE

A lion's roar is like a paint palette of colorful, creative words used to communicate with other lions. Picture God in heaven with a giant paint brush and beautiful colors. What on earth would He paint? Did you know God used His roar to paint the heavens and earth?

In the Bible, Genesis 1:1 (NIV) says, *In the beginning God created the heavens and the earth*. There was nothing to see until God spoke with His roar, *Let there be light* (Genesis 1:3, NIV). Then He spoke again and named the light day and the darkness night. He kept speaking until every detail of heaven and earth was created. Then God looked at what He had spoken and saw that it was good. Everything God spoke then and speaks now is good. A creative roar brings forth what is good.

Your roar can be creative too! Use your words to bring about something good, not bad. Speaking mean or hurtful things to someone or about someone isn't using your roar to create. It is using your roar to tear something down. Learn to use your roar to create joy, not sadness, in someone's life. Here is a positive/creative word bank lions use for building others up:

bravo, wow, super, terrific, cool, amazing, superb, brilliant, fantastic, fabulous, champion, tops, lovely, spot on, keep trying, well done, you rock, great job, tip top, good thinking, you can do it

Use your word bank and get ready to roar.

MY ROAR

Make your own creative word bank or add to this list. Begin using positive words around friends and family. Take one day and fast from negative, critical, harmful words. To fast means to stop doing something. So, for one day, don't let anything come out of your mouth except words from your word bank.

PONDERING PAWS

Talk to God about how you can be a lion and use creative words to build up others. Journal about your day without using negative words. How did it feel? Was it hard?

_____

_____

_____

_____

_____

_____

_____

_____

_____

_____

_____

_____

_____

_____

_____

_____

_____

LIONS LEAD

UNDER THE TREE

The lion is the most majestic creature in God's animal kingdom. Everything about a lion screams royalty. Its powerful-looking body and mane stand out. Add to that a kingly style and you have leadership. A lion holds its head up high and moves about with a fierce leading.

A lion has a strong personality and power that bring respect. A lion leads the animal kingdom because of its confidence. Just like a lion, God wants you to be a leader among people. Leaders are those with great courage, not showing fear. Kindness with confidence attracts others. Leaders do not gossip or join others in complaining. They find solutions to problems. You are not too young to be a leader.

You can be among God's young lion leaders in the Bible: David, Josiah, Daniel, Joseph, and more.
Now, get ready to roar!

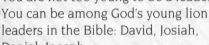

MY ROAR

Leaders don't complain; they solve problems. Ask God to show you something you have been complaining about. Then ask God for a solution to the problem. Do what He tells you to do.

PONDERING PAWS

Journal about the problem God showed you in *My Roar*.
Write out the problem and what you did about it.
Ask God to give you some traits of a leader. Write them down.

LIONS LISTEN

UNDER THE TREE

Listen up! Lions have super good hearing for stalking their prey. They just know when a yummy catch is hidden in dense grass. Moving, rotating ears allow them to hear without adjusting their bodies. Lions' ears swivel and spin as they go to the place of a sound. Lions' ears are like a built-in alert system.

Being alert is keeping your eyes and ears wide awake. It's being aware and ready to hear. God wants us to have moving ears too. At times, He wants to talk about life. Other times, He wants to warn us not to do something that might harm us. God also speaks to us about people we need to help or pray for. Our ears need to be alert and swivel to the source of God's voice.

One night, a missionary who worked in a dangerous country decided to take the long way home along the beach. The beaches in this country were not safe to walk after dark. But, she thought she could take big strides and make it home before dark. The missionary didn't make it home. Instead, she watched as the sun gently disappeared, and the moon brightly appeared.

In the sand just ahead of her, she noticed several footprints. Someone had run just up ahead of her. A bandit had been watching her and had set a trap on the path ahead of her. He ran from the bushes above the beach, pointing a gun at her. "Give me your money," he demanded. Frozen in fear, but alert, the woman heard a voice say, "Just drop your bag. He won't hurt you." It was the sweet voice of the Holy Spirit. Peace came over her! She dropped her bag, backing slowly away. The bandit snatched up the bag and disappeared into the night.

This was a lesson in alertness! Practice being a good listener. Cell phones and iPads are fun, but they can keep us from listening to family and clearly hearing God. Be an alert lion that listens, and get ready to roar.

MY ROAR

Pick a friend or family member. Ask them a question: What is your favorite fun thing to do? Why do you like to do it? Then listen! Practice listening to others without talking until they have finished.

PONDERING PAWS

Practice Listening to God

- Find a quiet place inside or outside your house.
- Set a timer and be quiet for 10 minutes.
- If stray thoughts come to you, write them down on paper and get them out of your mind. *Example of stray thoughts might be: I want to play baseball right now; I have homework; I need to call a friend, etc.*
- Once your mind is clear from random thoughts, listen for God to speak to you. Write down in your journal what you are hearing.

_____

_____

_____

_____

_____

_____

_____

_____

_____

_____

_____

_____

_____

_____

LIONS SIZE UP LIONS (PART 1)

CHEW ON THIS

Ears that hear and eyes that see—the LORD has made them both.
Proverbs 20:12 (NIV)

UNDER THE TREE

Size it up! At first, a lion's roar may sound like all other roars to human ears, but to lions they are not the same. Did you know lions can tell the size and kind of other lions by their roar? For example, mother lions sense the roar of a lion who might want to hurt their cubs. A roar can be a warning! Lions are good at sizing up kinds of lions by their roars.

What does this mean for me? We can size up and examine a person, place, or thing. It's important to investigate, separate, and study groups of kids, adults, and places. It's like when voters size up the candidates running for office. They are checking out honesty and character before voting. Sizing it up is observing someone or something to get information. It's watching situations and deciding how God wants us to move or act.

Hey, guys, don't be suspicious or afraid, but try to examine, judge, and size up situations. What do you sense if friends ask you to go to a "Haunted Hill House"? What do you sense, if at a friend's over-night, an R-rated movie is offered? What if an adult you don't know well takes an interest in you? Do you know how to size up what's happening in your space?

Pay attention to what you see, hear, and feel. Then you will be like a lion who sizes up other lions. Come along and get ready to roar.

MY ROAR

Size up a situation or group of friends in your life. Think ahead! Ask yourself, "What will I say or do if an R-rated movie is played at a friend's party?" Size it up!

PONDERING PAWS

Today, ask God if there is a situation or group of people He wants you to size up. Also, journal a situation when you made the mistake of not sizing things up. What was the effect?

LIONS SIZE UP LIONS (PART 2)

CHEW ON THIS

I baptize you with water, but he will baptize you with the Holy Spirit. *Mark 1:8 (NIV)*

UNDER THE TREE

Last time, we talked about lions who size things up. Lions discern the size and kind of other lions by their roars. God wants to teach us to be lion-like discerners.

God wants us to use the Knower He has placed inside of us. That Knower is the Holy Spirit! The Knower is a comforter and helper. He helps us size up the world around us. The Knower helps us recognize with special eyes what's wrong or right. What's great is that in the center of the Knower is God's love. That love shows compassion toward something or someone. Love hates evil and clings to a good God.

When do you need the Knower to size up a person, place, or thing? Here are some ideas to think about:

- TV commercials or programs. Good and bad things happen so quickly as you watch!
- People and places that feel unsafe or wrong.
- News and gossip.
- What you hear or see against God and the Bible on the news or by people running for political office.

A lion leader sizes up people, places, and things with love and truth. God wants us to be able to sense what He is saying and doing. Ask the Holy Spirit, the Knower, to come close and help you. Then, get ready to roar!

MY ROAR

First, ask the Holy Spirit to fill your heart with God's love. Then, read Acts 2. Focus your heart on Acts 2:2 (KJV) that says there came a rushing mighty wind. That means "a roar of the Spirit came." The Knower wants to roar through you.

PONDERING PAWS

Write about people, places, or things where you remember feeling "unsafe" or icky. How do you plan to react next time?
Write out your plan to let the Knower help you.

LIONS ARE BRAVE

CHEW ON THIS

Have I not commanded you? Be strong and courageous.
Do not be afraid; do not be discouraged, for the LORD your God
will be with you wherever you go.

Joshua 1:9 (NIV)

UNDER THE TREE

Lions are one of our best symbols of bravery. They're one of the only creatures that will take on animals bigger than they are. Lions will hunt some of the most dangerous animals. They are our symbol of courage, boldness, and power. So, when someone says you have the heart of a lion, it means you're brave. Even a child can have the heart of a lion. Here is an example of a child with the heart of a lion. He is considered brave.

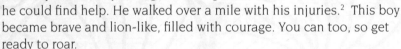

A 6-year-old boy named Tyler Moon went quad biking with his dad. Their day did not go as expected. Tyler and his father went off the path and found themselves in a bad accident. They crashed their bikes, and both suffered harmful injuries. The father was unconscious while Tyler remained awake, but injured with broken ribs. Like a lion's roar, something rose up inside Tyler when he saw his dad was hurt. The young boy knew he had to overcome fear and help his dad. Tyler began walking to where he could find help. He walked over a mile with his injuries.[2] This boy became brave and lion-like, filled with courage. You can too, so get ready to roar.

MY ROAR

Step out and do one brave thing this week. It might be as simple as reading a book report aloud in class. It could also be doing something that risks failure.

PONDERING PAWS

Talk to God about your fears and areas where you need to be lion-like.

_____

_____

_____

_____

_____

_____

_____

_____

_____

_____

_____

_____

_____

_____

_____

_____

_____

_____

_____

THE LION IN JESUS

UNDER THE TREE

Who is Jesus to you? Jesus is often called "the lion of the tribe of Judah." Jesus is like a lion in many ways. He is our strong, true, and ultimate King forever, and He is over everything. Jesus is strong, and the Bible tells us He is King over His Church. How is Jesus like a lion to us?

Lions have strong teeth and paws. Jesus' words in Scripture are life-giving, timeless, and powerful. Lions are fearless! At times, they are frightening and protective of their families and lion friends. Jesus was kind, but we have to remember that His power is to be respected. He is protective of you! Just as we respect our parents' authority over us, we honor Jesus' authority over us.

Lion-like children will put their trust in Jesus and answer to Him. Jesus is described in the Bible with lion-like features—He is strong and fearless in protecting His own. Are you His own? An Old Testament scripture, Amos 3:8 (NIV), says, The lion has roared—who will not fear? The Lion, Jesus, makes God's enemy run away and scatter. The devil is afraid of lion-likeness. A lion's traits are worth chasing because they are also Jesus-like. Be a lion and get ready to roar.

MY ROAR

If you have not received the roaring Lion as your friend, Lord, and Savior, pray this prayer with a family member:

Lord Jesus Christ, I believe that You took the pain of the cross. You died to give me new life. I ask You to come into my life and to give me Your peace and joy. I am sorry for doing what I want to do, when I want to do it. I have gone my own way and have done wrong. Please forgive me for doing wrong. I receive You now as my Lord and Savior. Please fill me with the love of God and Your Holy Spirit. Help me to follow You and to serve You all my life.

Thank You, Jesus. Amen.

PONDERING PAWS

Draw a picture of a lion. Write down those traits of the lion that already fit you. Then write those traits you want to grow in. How does a lion remind you of what you know about Jesus?

PART TWO

MY DESTINY DEN

The Lion Within

Great job, guys! Now that you've finished *Gettin' Ready to Roar*, let's keep prowling through God's Word in *My Destiny Den*. Come on! Let's go! Lions search, roam, stroll, and wander through the tall grasslands. They can leap 36 feet in the air. You've taken the leap from the starting gate into the lion's destiny den. Destiny is God's perfectly chosen purpose for you. He has chosen you to be part of His special plan in history. The destiny den will take you into a special place with Him. You're an original lion, made to leap far and high as you grow closer to God.

FINDING THE LION WITHIN

CHEW ON THIS

So if you sinful people know how to give good gifts to your children, how much more will your heavenly Father give the Holy Spirit to those who ask him. *Luke* 11:13 (NLT)

UNDER THE TREE

Are you a treasure hunter? Want to find treasure that is hidden inside you? People love hunting for treasure in the most unusual places. Using a metal detector (finder), a father and son once found a Viking treasure. They hit a mother lode of silver and gold, said to have been worth one million dollars.[3] Jewelry, watches, and coins have been found under sand on beaches. Playgrounds, parks, schoolyards, ball fields, and picnic areas are places to find treasure.

A metal detector is a long metal stick. When it's turned on, the bottom acts as a magnet. The magnet scans the surrounding ground in search of metal, such as gold. If something is discovered, a sound alerts the searcher of its presence. Knowing Jesus allows the Holy Spirit to plant treasure within us. The Holy Spirit is like a metal detector that attracts those gifts and treasures buried within you. Holy Spirit power, turned on, finds that treasure. God wants to use that lion treasure within you to help people. Check out the Lion Within List below to see what some of those treasures from 1 Corinthians 12:7–10 include.

LION WITHIN LIST

Wise Thoughts—People come to me with problems, and I have good answers for them.

Knowledge—I know things about people's past and present before they tell me.

Faith/Believing—I have strong beliefs about what's right and wrong.

Healing—I love praying for sick people to be healed.

Wonders—Special things God can do like bringing the dead to life. I am interested in the wonders of God.

Hearing God—I love listening for God to speak to me in prayer. I also love to speak God's encouragement to people.

You are God's treasure, and you were born to roar!

MY ROAR

Chew on the Lion Within List. Which ones fit you? When you find the one that fits, go use it with a friend or family member.

PONDERING PAWS

Do any of these treasures on the list fit you? Write them in your journal and talk to God about how to use them with your friends.

LOVABLE LIONS

CHEW ON THIS

The LORD appeared to us in the past, saying: "I have loved you with an everlasting love; I have drawn you with unfailing kindness."

Jeremiah 31:3 (NIV)

UNDER THE TREE

Lovable lions know they are received and loved by a forgiving father. In Luke 15:11–32, Jesus told a story about two brothers who had a loving father. The father had stored up a lifetime of his boys' allowances. Each week they were given a small portion for doing their chores. The older son was responsible! He knew that receiving his share weekly would make his money last longer. He would not be tempted to spend it all at once and in one place.

However, the younger brother asked the father to give him all of his allowance at once. He did not want to wait. He thought he was hot stuff because he had lots of money to spend. He took the money and ran away from home! New friends liked him because of all his money. But, as he began to spend it foolishly, those friends ran away from him. Before he knew it, he was all alone with no money, no friends, no food…nothing.

He began to miss his family. He realized how foolish he had been to leave and decided to return home. He had given up his right to his allowance and spent it all, but he thought maybe his father would take him back as a servant boy. At least, he would have food to eat. He also was afraid that by running away he had given up his right to be his father's son. That thought made him feel sad and empty inside.

To his surprise, as he started up the road toward home, his father recognized him. From far away the father ran to greet him. Even though the son had done wrong, the father still loved him. He was welcomed home and treated as if nothing ever happened. The son was given new shoes and a new coat by his father.

You are a lovable lion. Even when you do wrong, you are loved and accepted by Father God. You were born to roar!

MY ROAR

Close your eyes and picture Jesus. Then, picture yourself running to Him and letting Him wrap His arms around you in a big bear hug.

PONDERING PAWS

Do you believe you are forgiven and loved by God? Journal those things in the story that showed the young son was loved by his father. Then journal the ways God shows you that He loves you.

KITTY CAT TO LION

CHEW ON THIS

But you are a chosen people, a royal priesthood, a holy nation, God's special possession, that you may declare the praises of him who called you out of darkness into his wonderful light.

1 Peter 2:9 (NIV)

UNDER THE TREE

When you look in the mirror, do you see a kitty cat or a lion? You were born to be lion-like, not kitty-like. Do you believe you are strong and powerful for God?

When you asked Jesus into your heart, you immediately moved from kitty to lion. You also received keys of power and authority. What's also amazing is that you are now part of a royal family of lions. You are a royal son or daughter of the King of all creation. Jesus said, *All authority has been given to Me in heaven and on earth* (Matthew 28:18, NASB). His kingdom is yours too! You are now included in Father God's big plan to spread His kingdom everywhere. No matter how old you are, you can rule as royalty.

Through Jesus' life, the devil has been defeated, but sin and darkness are still in the world. Hatred, sickness, bad people, wars, and poverty are all around us. The good news is you are now a lion, not a kitty cat any longer. You can help destroy sin and darkness in the world. Fighting with the light of love and standing up for what's right replaces darkness. As you live for Jesus, darkness around you must become light.

So, do you see a lion when you look in the mirror? Is there a roar within you? The roar carries God's peace and goodness. It carries promises and a love that is very powerful. You have the ability to share about Jesus and change people's lives. Amazing things can happen when you are a son or daughter of the King. When you know you are a lion, the devil bows to Jesus when you walk into a room. You were born to roar!

MY ROAR

Go stand in front of a mirror. Say, "I am one of God's lions, and I am a world changer."

PONDERING PAWS

Sit with God and ponder what Jesus did for you.
Write about what you saw when you looked into the mirror.
Do you believe you are strong and powerful for God?

FEARLESS

UNDER THE TREE

Jamie loved playing with most of the kids on the block. But, there was one boy named Alex who could be really mean, and at times Jamie was afraid of him. Alex was a bully who daily picked on Jamie over his faith in God.

"There is no God!" Alex would say in his taunting voice. "You're a goody-two-shoes! Christians are weak!" he said. Jamie hated being around Alex, but there was something inside Jamie that felt sorry for Alex. One day, Alex was taunting and teasing Jamie. Suddenly, a Bible verse came to Jamie's mind, *If your brother or sister sins, go and point out their fault, just between the two of you* (Matthew 18:15, NIV).

Jamie sprang into action! "Why do you pick on Jesus? Aren't you tired of being mean?" Jamie asked. "Jesus loves you and died for you, even when you are mean to Him." At that moment, Jamie felt like a lion for Jesus. Alex was silent! The expression on his face changed, and he began to cry. Jamie felt Jesus' love for Alex and put an arm around him. Once Alex stopped crying, he asked Jamie to tell him more about Jesus. He also asked, "How can I know Jesus?" He promised never to bully anyone else again.

You see, boldness comes from knowing God's Word. Don't hold back! Be fearless like a lion because you were born to roar!

MY ROAR
If you don't read your Bible daily, begin today. Set out to become fearless like Jamie! Invite a friend to church or try to share with a friend how Jesus has made a difference in your life.

PONDERING PAWS

Ask God for a Bible verse that He wants you to read today.
Wait for an answer, then look up the verse. Has anyone bullied you
because you want to follow Jesus? Talk to God about it here and forgive
them. If you are really afraid, tell an adult!

ROARING WITH PURPOSE

CHEW ON THIS

"For I know the plans that I have for you," declares the LORD, "plans for welfare and not for calamity to give you a future and a hope." *Jeremiah* 29:11 (NASB)

UNDER THE TREE

Alex spun the globe on the desk in the bedroom. The world seemed like a scary place. A thought came to Alex's mind, "I sure hope my cousins are safe." Alex's two cousins, aunt, and uncle were missionaries in a place on the verge of civil war. In the middle of the night, they had to flee to a neighboring country. The war came so quickly, they left with only the clothes on their backs. They had escaped just before the threatening gunfire began.

Alex's mom appeared in the bedroom doorway. "What are you doing?" she asked. "I'm thinking about my cousins," said Alex. "I know what you mean," replied Mom. "I have been praying for them. They love Jesus more than their own lives. They decided to follow Him no matter the cost. Everyone has a purpose in life. Their purpose is to share the gospel in a dark place, but danger goes with that purpose." Mom continued, "You're always safe in the center of God's plans and purposes."

Alex plopped face down upon the bed. "What is my purpose?" he asked. Mom laughed. "As you grow and seek Him with all your heart, it will become apparent." "Do I have to go far away like my cousins to have purpose?" asked Alex. "No, not at all!" smiled Mom. "Your purpose in God can be found at school, among friends, or even in sports. His plan and purpose for us is perfect. He will show you! But, in the meantime, reach out for purpose now. You can start by loving your family and making a difference at school and even in the world."

Alex was relieved. "I guess you're right, Mom. I never thought of that before. I know I should be nicer to my little brother." "That's a great start," laughed Mom. "While you're thinking about being a world changer, clean your room." Don't forget, you were born to roar!

MY ROAR

God's plan and purpose for you may change as you grow older. Ask God to show you your purpose now. Here are some ideas on finding purpose now:

- *Help your mom or dad with a chore you would not normally do.*
- *Help an elderly neighbor with their yard, groceries, etc.*
- *Start a prayer club in your school or an afterschool prayer club at home.*
- *Earn money for a charity or someone in need.*

PONDERING PAWS

Ask Jesus a question about Himself.
The start of finding purpose is in knowing Jesus as a true friend.
Once you know Him, you will find purpose for living.

BEING LIONHEARTED

CHEW ON THIS

I praise you because I am fearfully and wonderfully made;
your works are wonderful, I know that full well.
Psalm 139:14 (NIV)

UNDER THE TREE

Eleven-year-old twins Liam and Emma flipped through the pages of an old family album. Their baby pictures were always amusing to them. Liam was born first, and he loved reminding Emma that he was the older of the two.

"Look, Mom," said Emma, smiling so pleased as she pointed to one of her baby pictures. "See my little face, Mom. Wasn't I sweet?" Liam rolled his eyes at her. "Wasn't I *sweet*?" he mimicked. "You're still sweet," said Mom. "You are just as wonderful today as the day you were born. Liam and Emma, just look at your little feet, ears, and fingers. God made you twins, but you are so different from each other and anyone else." Mom pointed to the little mole on Emma's left toe in one picture. "You still have that cute mole on your toe, Emma," she said.

"Yes, it's still there, Mom, and I don't like it. It's ugly. I think it was a big mistake," said Emma. "God doesn't make mistakes," said Mom. "God put that mole on your toe, and it's a part of who you are. It's like a little kiss mark. I can't think of anything more wonderfully made than our bodies." Mom wrapped her arms around her twins. "God must have something really special planned for your lives. He is giving you both an important assignment in His plans. Your life is very important to the world around you." Mom kept hugging her twins. "Just keep listening to God, and He will direct your steps."

We are perfect because God made us, and we are important in His eyes. We're called to be the sons and daughters of a King. That alone makes us unique and born to roar.

MY ROAR

Find someone at school or in your neighborhood who needs encouragement. Have you noticed anyone who is often alone, sad, or outcast? Can you include them in your friendships?

PONDERING PAWS

Share with God anything in your life that is difficult. Is there something you wish you could change about yourself? Talk to Him about it!

NO LION IS ALIKE

CHEW ON THIS

The lion has roared—who will not fear?
The Sovereign LORD has spoken—who can but prophesy?
Amos 3:8 (NIV)

UNDER THE TREE

Did you ever wonder why lions roar? It's not really a mystery. Animal scientists and lion watchers around the world have discovered the answers. Do you want to know why lions roar? First, lions are very protective of their homes. The male lion's main job is to defend his pride (family). The roar warns away any animals that might harm the lion's family.

Have you ever had to protect a little brother or sister from harm? Have you stood up for a friend who was being treated badly? Protection is a type of roar.

It's important to know different kinds of roars. We need to be warned about God's enemies as well. Some enemies are fear, unforgiveness, unkindness, anger, rebellion, jealousy, hatred, and more. Roaring a big NO to issues in life that weigh us down can protect us from evil.

Second, lions roar just to talk to one another. No lions are alike; each lion's roar creates a different sound. That means that each lion can be known by its own special voice. God created each of us to have a distinctive way of speaking. Our fingerprint is different than anyone else's in the world. God made us to be set apart from anyone else. So, our personality, our looks, and our voice are meant to be one-of-a-kind. Who we are and what we do is our roar. It can be seen and heard everywhere we go and in everything we do. God wants all that we are to represent all that He is. You were born to roar!

MY ROAR

Use your unique roar to help out a friend.
Pray for a friend who is sad or needs
encouragement.

PONDERING PAWS

Is there anything weighing you down that you would like to talk to God about? Ask God to tell you how you are marked by Him in a special way. Wait for an answer and write what you hear.

A LION ORIGINAL

CHEW ON THIS

For we are God's handiwork, created in Christ Jesus to do good works, which God prepared in advance for us to do. *Ephesians* 2:10 (NIV)

UNDER THE TREE

What does an original painting versus a copy look like? How can you tell if something is an original or a fake? A magnifying glass and good light are needed. But, be sure! An original is unique, matchless, rare, and one-of-a-kind. You are a lion original! God doesn't make fakes or copies. You are a creative, unique masterpiece of your Creator. You can know you are God's loved original. Knowing how and why God made you is important. He made you to love Him and be known by Him. God put something special inside you; that's so you can do something extraordinary in His name. Think of your creation as a beautiful painting by Father God. So, here are the four parts to how God makes lion originals. That's what you are!

RECOGNIZING A LION ORIGINAL

1. The Frame: Jesus, the carpenter, made a custom-built frame for God the Father to paint you upon. Jesus was even there when God created you. Colossians 1:16 (NIV) tells us, *For in him all things were created: things in heaven and on earth, visible and invisible.*

2. The Canvas: Original paintings are most often painted on a canvas, panel, paper, or wood. The canvas God used to create you was made from Himself. That means that we have personality traits like God's. We are not gods, but we are like our Father in many ways.

3. The Painting: You are God's painting! Artists sketch out their ideas before they begin to paint. God sketched you out way before He created you. Psalm 139:13 (NIV) says, *You created my inmost being; you knit me together in my mother's womb.* An original carries the signature of the creator. You are marked by God. His name is written upon your life.

4. The Back of the Painting: Originals have tags on the back that tell the painting's story. God wants to tell a story about you. Put your life into His hands and under His paintbrush.

Never forget—you were born to roar!

MY ROAR

Step out from your painting. Name one thing that is special inside you (Example: smart, good in sports, a good friend, musical, or healer of people in Jesus' name). NOW, act upon it!

PONDERING PAWS

Make a tag about yourself that would go on God's painting of you.
Talk to God! Put on the tag what He calls you.

LAUGHING AT LIES

UNDER THE TREE

Sometimes we just have to laugh at the lies of the devil. He has nothing new to say or do. He can't create anything new. The devil can only take God's works and try to change them into his works. That's how he fools people. He wants to fool you with lies because He is the father of lies. The word for "devil" means "faultfinder, accuser." His name also means "to ridicule" or "to gnaw and bite at." When the devil lies, he is doing what comes easy for him. You have to laugh at him. Ha, ha, ha, ha! He wants to fill your lion ears with lies about yourself. Will you let him, or will you laugh at him? Lions just laugh at lies!

So, how do you recognize the devil's lies? First, you have to know the God who speaks truth. Know what God says about you. He says you are loved, forgiven, and a daughter or son. God says He loves you in your bad, sad, and happy times. He doesn't always like what you do, but He loves you. When mistakes are made, the devil will try to whisper into your ear that you're dumb, clumsy, bad, worthless, or worse. Be lion-like and stand courageous against the devil's lies. Let your lion's claws swat lies before they land. Don't let lies land in your heart or mind. Pay attention to what you let come into your ears. Be lion-like and laugh at the lies of the devil because you were born to roar.

MY ROAR

Let God search your heart for lies you have believed about yourself. Let Him pull them out. Replace each of those lies with truth statements about you.

PONDERING PAWS

Journal the list of lies you have believed about yourself.
(*Example: I am not smart, I am ugly, I am not talented, I this, I that*).
Replace these lies with a list of things that are true about you.

GOTTA HAVE COURAGE

CHEW ON THIS

Be strong and courageous. Do not be afraid or terrified because of them, for the LORD your God goes with you; he will never leave you nor forsake you.

Deuteronomy 31:6 (NIV)

UNDER THE TREE

You gotta have COURAGE! The Cowardly Lion in the movie, *The Wizard of Oz*, wanted courage. The adorable, but frightened, lion joined the journey to see the Wizard. Most lions are known to be fierce and are called "king of the beasts," but the Cowardly Lion in the movie walked in self-doubt and timidity. He didn't understand what it means to walk fearlessly like other lions. When Cowardly Lion meets Dorothy and friends, his lion instincts are held back by fear. Overcoming fear takes courage! Courage requires us to take action in the face of our fear.

Kids with courage face their fears head-on. The lion in the *Wizard of* Oz faced his fear of a wicked witch. In the end, the great Wizard gave the lion a gold medal. On the medal was carved the word "courage." His keepsake of courage affirmed the lion within him. God's medals and keepsakes from His Word affirm the lion within us. God loves us and wants us to know who we are. Walking through our fear can take away the fear. If you fear reading a book report in front of your class, do it. If you fear trying out for a sports team, do it. If you fear the dark, go into it. If you fear trying something new, do it. We all have fear, but let God turn fear into courage. Remember, you were born to roar.

MY ROAR

Pick one thing you are afraid of. Take steps to walk into it and through it. Sometimes it takes pushing through your fear more than once. Picture Jesus holding your hand or standing beside you.

PONDERING PAWS

Look up scriptures on courage, finding God's medals and keepsakes within His Word. Journal to God about your greatest fears. Allow Him to impart courage into those places of fear.

ACCESS YOUR POWER CLAWS

UNDER THE TREE

If you had feet like a lion, your front paws would be great for gripping. But, the real power of the lion's paws is in the claws. Relaxing, resting lions hide the claws inside their paws. Positioned and ready to strike, the lion's claws pop right out. It's like keeping a sword inside the cover until it's needed in battle.[4] Pretend you have lion claws! Make a closed fist, and then suddenly, open your hand, extending your fingers outward. That's what a lion's claw is like.

Lions have control as to when to use or not to use their sharp claws. They know how to access their powerful tools when needed. We too have access to something powerful in our lives. Our power comes through the work of the Holy Spirit. The Holy Spirit always holds hands with Jesus. When we receive Jesus as Lord and Savior, something happens. The Holy Spirit comes with Jesus to work in and through us.

Power claws in our life are the gifts of the Holy Spirit. His gifts pop out of us when we are positioned to serve others. The Holy Spirit lets us know when we are to say something kind or keep silent in a situation. Remember, a lion's claws are in the paw when the lion is at rest. We walk at rest with the Holy Spirit inside us until He wants us to do or say something special for God. That's when the Holy Spirit comes out through us because we were born to roar.

MY ROAR

The Holy Spirit lets us decide when to use His power. He doesn't make us serve God. Watch for a place to access and release Holy Spirit power.

(*Examples: Pray for someone who is sick and needs to be healed. Pray encouragement over someone sad. Help someone in need, mow an elderly neighbor's lawn, etc.*)

PONDERING PAWS

Sit with God! Invite the Holy Spirit to come close. Make a picture of a lion's paw with claws. Above each claw, write down one thing that the Holy Spirit might do through you. Use Galatians 5:22–23 for help.

_____

_____

_____

_____

_____

_____

_____

_____

_____

_____

_____

_____

_____

_____

_____

_____

_____

_____

HARNESSED LIONS (PART 1)

UNDER THE TREE

There was a king driving his carriage throughout his kingdom. The carriage was edged in gold, with stunning carvings upon it. Six large lions pulled the beautiful coach. But, one day, something broke under the carriage. The lions stopped moving. The king crawled under the carriage to fix what was broken. As he lay on his back, the last two lions' paws rested close by. If a lion should kick him or pop out its claws at him, it could kill him. A startled lion could cause the carriage to run over him.

But, the king wasn't afraid. He trusted the very lions he had disciplined and trained. They would not move one inch unless he told them to. You see, each of the king's lions was harnessed. A harness is a set of straps by which an animal is fastened to a cart, plow, or carriage. Harnessing allows an animal to be controlled by the driver. The harness works to teach the animal to obey its king and master.

God is our King and carriage driver. Will you let His love harness and train you to His voice and to His ways? Wow! We get to follow and submit our hearts and minds to God. The king trusted his harnessed lions. Let God harness you into trusting Him because you were born to roar.

MY ROAR

Be a harnessed lion! Pick an area where God can trust you to make a good choice. Then do it!

PONDERING PAWS

Journal your own harnessed list of areas in your life where God wants you to trust Him more. Journal areas in your life where you are harnessed to Him.
(*Example: I obey my teacher at school.*)

HARNESSED LIONS (PART 2)

UNDER THE TREE

Two young lions raced across an open field, flicking their tails. The two looked back and saw the six adult lions harnessed to the king's carriage. The young lions called out to them, "Join us in the shade. See the yummy meat we are feeding on? Drink from streams of cool water." The majestic lions didn't reply or respond in any way. The young lions couldn't understand why they stood quietly, waiting for their king's voice.

Suddenly, a rope fell around the necks of the two young lions. They were led off to the king's court for training and discipline. Being steered away from the freedom of green pastures made them sad. Surrounded with brown dirt and high fences, the king began to work with them. Lovingly using his whip and bridle, the king began to teach them to listen and obey.

They didn't know the king's training would make them strong and powerful. It felt so horrid. So much so, that one of the lions rebelled under the training. "This is not for me," he said proudly. "I like my freedom, green hills, and flowing streams." So, he found a way out by jumping the fence. Happily, he ran back to the green meadows. With sadness, the king let him go and did not chase after him.

The remaining lion decided to stay in the kingdom. He submitted his will to learn the ways of the king. As he grew, he discovered how to obey the slightest word from the king. In the end, he joined the team of lions pulling the king's carriage. He became one of the most powerful lions in the kingdom. Sadly, the disobedient lion fell into weakness. He never became powerful like other lions.[5]

You're meant to be like the obedient lion who became the most powerful. You were born to roar!

MY ROAR

Do you have trouble trusting and obeying adults?
Is there any area where your heart says "no" to God?
Practice "yes" in an area of your life where your feelings want to say "no."

PONDERING PAWS

God gives us a choice to disobey or submit. If you don't know if you are defiant, then ask God. Journal what He tells you.

_____
_____
_____
_____
_____
_____
_____
_____
_____
_____
_____
_____
_____
_____
_____
_____
_____
_____
_____
_____

WHAT'S MY THING?

CHEW ON THIS

All who are skilled among you are to come and make everything the LORD has commanded.

Exodus 35:10 (NIV)

UNDER THE TREE

"Every day! Just doin' that thing you do!" Those were the words in the title song for a movie, *That Thing You Do*. If someone asked you, "What's your thing?", what would you say? What are some things you like to do? What are some things you do well?

In the Bible there was one thing a boy named David liked to do. That one thing was to skillfully use a slingshot! The slingshot was one of the most important weapons in Bible times. David was a natural. The tribe David came from was known for being a select group of slingers. Judges 20:16 (NIV) says, *Among all these soldiers there were seven hundred select troops who were left-handed, each of whom could sling a stone at a hair and not miss.* David was talented at aiming the stones at the enemy's face and head. He could sling a stone 60 miles per hour. His natural ability for slinging was apparent to many.[6]

Each of us is born with skills and talents to help others. With our natural abilities, we can bring God's kingdom to earth. It's fun to use what we can do for God's glory. It's even more fun when the Holy Spirit runs alongside our talents and skills. They're even better when we give them to the Holy Spirit. Our greatest skills from God are amazing, and we were born to roar.

MY ROAR

What is a natural gift and skill God has given you?
Pray and dedicate that gift to God.
Next time you use it, thank the Holy Spirit for
allowing you to partner with Him in using the gift.

PONDERING PAWS

Write a note to God, thanking Him for your natural talents and gifts.
Write to His Holy Spirit, thanking Him for the gifts He gives as well.
(Remember your Lion Within List on page 40?) Think about the
difference between the gifts of the Holy Spirit and your talents.

LIONS SEE WELL

UNDER THE TREE

Let's learn a new lion fact. The lion's eyesight is amazing! Lions can see as well as you do during the day, but at night their eyesight is better by far than ours. Lions see almost ten times better in the darkness than humans. For the lion, it's like wearing night goggles and seeing in blue and green. Their night vision goes above and beyond what they see in the daytime.[7] When we dare to imagine a world beyond the one we can see, God provides a way for us to see in the dark.

God vision, which is our lion-like vision, is more than looking with the natural eyes. It's using imagination, daydreams, and inspired ideas. God-like vision is sort of a map God uses to show us many things we can do. Vision is a series of God-given ideas that help us to be creative and do great things for God. Ask God for vision for yourself and the things you can do. Be a world changer by grabbing God's vision, because you were born to roar.

MY ROAR

Materials Needed
- Old magazines
- Glue and scissors
- Large piece of poster board

Ask God to give you creative vision for the coming year. What special, fun things can you do for Him? Make a poster that shows some of the things you think God wants you to do.

PONDERING PAWS

Sit with God. Ask Him to give you vision for something you can do for Him this very year. Write about it! Use it in the *My Roar* activity.

A MOVIE REVIEW: THE LION KING

UNDER THE TREE

So…have you seen the movie, *The Lion King*? Did you know that God can use movies to speak to us? In this story of a young lion named Simba, we find many life lessons. Let's do a movie review. *The Lion King* is all about overcoming and taking your place in God's kingdom. It's about making a difference and being who you were created to be. Simba, the young lion, is challenged through the sad loss of his father. At first, he forgets he was created in the image of his father, Mufasa. We too can allow sad things to make us forget God, our heavenly Father. The devil can take advantage of our broken hearts.

Another character, Scar, is the bad lion in the movie. He gets Simba to believe he was the cause of Mufasa's death. Just like Scar, Satan uses traps to shame us. He makes us believe lies about our past, present, and future. Cruel Scar lets Simba take the blame for Mufasa's death. We also see how Satan can trick others into blaming us for their bad behavior. When we make simple mistakes, he likes to whisper that we are bad. But, God helps us face our mistakes and forgive ourselves through the love of Jesus Christ.

Simba realizes who he is and his purpose as a son of Mufasa. He discovers how to walk in the footsteps of his father. You can know that you belong to God, and then walk in His Son Jesus' footsteps. Once Simba's life was put in order, he made right choices. When our life is given over to Jesus, then we can make right choices.

Last of all, Simba learns the true value of friendship in Nala, Timon, and Pumbaa. He found friends who would not abandon him—just like how Jesus promises to never leave or forsake us. Remember, God created us to roar!

MY ROAR

Rent and watch *The Lion King* (even if you have already seen it). Use the checklist below to listen and find these wise quotes as you watch the movie.

- *"There's more to being king than getting your way all the time."* Mufasa
- *"Everything light touches is our kingdom. Everything light touches will be yours."* Mufasa
- *"What about that shadowy place?"* Simba; *"You must never go there."* Mufasa
- *"Remember who you are. He lives in you."* Rafiki
- *"You have forgotten who you are, so you have forgotten me. You must take your place. Remember who you are. You are my son and the one true king."* Mufasa
- *"You are more than you have become; you must take your place."* Mufasa
- *"Being brave doesn't mean you go looking for trouble."* Mufasa

PONDERING PAWS

Pick one of the quotes from *My Roar*. Talk to God
about the meaning of the quote in your life.

LIONS WHO DREAM

UNDER THE TREE

Do you dream at night? Our night dreams can be from God! Sometimes He just wants to get our attention. Sleeping is the one time during the day when we are still, quiet, and listening. That's when God can get through to us.

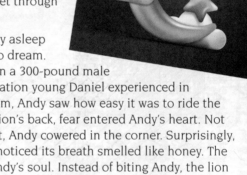

Twelve-year-old Andy fell soundly asleep and within moments he began to dream. In the dream, Andy was sitting on a 300-pound male lion in a cage, similar to the situation young Daniel experienced in Daniel 6 in the Bible. In the dream, Andy saw how easy it was to ride the lion. But, when slipping off the lion's back, fear entered Andy's heart. Not sure what the lion would do next, Andy cowered in the corner. Surprisingly, the lion let out a big roar. Andy noticed its breath smelled like honey. The roar brought joy and peace to Andy's soul. Instead of biting Andy, the lion snuggled his mane into Andy's face. Suddenly, Andy was back in bed and safely in his familiar room.

What do you think God was telling Andy through the dream? Maybe seeing a lion in a dream means Jesus is nearby. That's because Jesus is often represented by a lion. Also, the roar in the dream may be telling Andy to speak out in Jesus' name. The honey smell of the lion's breath could mean Jesus is sweet and kind. God wants Andy to be sweet and kind like Jesus when he speaks the truth. God may be saying strength, courage, and majesty are qualities found in Jesus. He wants Andy to know he can have those qualities too. Similarly, riding the lion could show Andy that talent comes through a journey with Jesus. You also can learn what God wants for you from Andy's dream. Remember, you were born to roar!

MY ROAR
Talk to your friends and share your dreams. As you share, help each other to hear what God is saying through your dreams.

PONDERING PAWS

Journal a dream that stands out to you as a God dream. Ask God what He wants to tell you about your dream and journal it.

A LION'S HEART

UNDER THE TREE

Have you heard of the movie series, *Star Trek*? One of the main characters is Doctor Benjamin Spock. He's an alien with pointy ears, and he comes from the planet Vulcan. Vulcans aren't born to share their feelings. They even call emotions foolishness. We know the story of Spock is make-believe because God created people to have real feelings.

Feelings are emotions that come from the center of our heart. Some are positive like happiness and joy. Others are negative like anger, sadness, anxiety, and loneliness. You can probably think of even more feelings you have experienced in your life.

God is an expert on emotions because He created them. He knows what we are feeling before we feel it. He wants to enable us to spot bad feelings when they appear. Bad feelings need to be shared with someone because it helps to talk things out. For example, negative, growly, grouchy feelings mean we have hurts hidden in our hearts. Negative feelings can be God's way of warning us about hurts in our hearts that need to be healed. So, it's important to tell someone.

Sharing with family or a friend can release God's healing grace. Since the word "grace" can mean power, it's God's power that heals our hurt. God's grace can also help us have courage to talk with someone about our feelings. God is preparing you for something very exciting. You are valuable to God, your King.

It's never wrong to have bad feelings. It is wrong to hide them and to hurt others because of them. Don't be a Vulcan; pay attention to your feelings! Find a friend or parent you can share your heart with, and remember God always has a listening ear. It's not helpful to hide your feelings. Sharing your feelings is a type of roaring. It's a way of letting Jesus know who you are—even though He already knows!

MY ROAR
Ask God if there is one bad feeling that keeps coming to you. Talk to a friend or family member about it. Don't hide it!

PONDERING PAWS

Create your own Feelings Board. Make a list of words you know that describe feelings. Throughout the year, continue to add words to your board. Circle ones you struggle with most and continue to talk to God about them.

PART THREE
LION SAYINGS

Cool God Growls

You are doing great, guys! Let's keep up the good work! There are hundreds of ways for you to get to your lion destiny. The most direct path to your roar is through knowing Jesus and asking Him to give you the power to make good choices. Good choices made each day can turn what's ordinary into something extraordinary. We are going to spend some time now learning fun and cool sayings from the Bible. Many people use these sayings every day, yet they don't know they're from God's Word. As you read, let them help you speed up your journey into your roar. Allow these phrases to make you more lion-like.

FIGHT THE GOOD FIGHT

CHEW ON THIS

Fight the good fight of the faith. 1 Timothy 6:12 (NIV)

UNDER THE TREE

The word "fight" means combat, battle, to stand up against something or someone and more. A good fight is a fair fight that doesn't include hitting or punching. A fight is good when it's done Jesus' way.

Jesus was a fighter who carried in His heart the good fight message! He used His voice and His Father's invisible weapons to fight many battles. Jesus fought with the roar of words to protect God's plans and purposes. His anger was not as much toward people as it was toward what people did.

Jesus has always fought against bad ideas and wrong beliefs. His friends, the disciples, took action to fight for what they believed. One way to fight the good fight was to speak truth where others spoke lies. Each of Jesus' 12 friends had to fight for what was right within their hearts. The disciples' fight turned the world upside down. Your fight for something good and right can make a difference too.

So, when we say "fight the good fight," it means fight for what Jesus taught. You must be sure in your heart of what is right and worth fighting for. Let's make a fight list of what Jesus' friends fought for. Read Matthew 5:1–11 and the Jesus Fight List below:

JESUS FIGHT LIST

Humility – Think positively about yourself, but just don't think about yourself too often. Think of others!

Mourning – It's feeling sad over the things that make God sad. As you get closer to God, you learn what hurts His heart. When we feel sad, God promises to comfort us.

Meekness – It's standing out, but not showing off. It's letting people see Jesus in us when we do something important.

Hunger and Thirst for What's Right – Have you ever been really hungry and thirsty? This means having a strong desire to do what is right in God's eyes.

Merciful – To have mercy is to be loving and kind to others. It's feeling sorry for someone the way that God would.

Pure in Heart – This is a heart that is not offended by others or stays mad at them. It is a heart that goes to God when we do wrong and asks Him for forgiveness.

Peacemaker – This is someone who makes peace, rather than starts fights. It's helping others to get along.

Fight the good fight because you were born to roar.

MY ROAR

Pick two entries from Jesus' fight list that you intend to work on. Do something using the list that shows you fought a good fight.

PONDERING PAWS

Talk to God about things on the Jesus Fight List that you need to work on. Talk to Him about something on the list you have done well. Pray for opportunities to "fight the good fight" using the list.

SUFFER FOOLS GLADLY

UNDER THE TREE

Let's play the Backwards Game! Try to say these words backwards: super bowl, popsicle, snow and rain. Sometimes God likes to say things in a backwards way to get our attention, like "suffer fools gladly"! That means to joyfully suffer with patience around foolish people. God is saying to be patient around those who say and do foolish things. It's tempting to be annoyed by those who act careless and unwise. God says to be careful how you respond to foolish words and deeds. So, what is the difference between being foolish and wise? This chart shows how a fool compares to a wise person:

FOOLISH	WISE
"I'm always right, and don't listen to adults."	"I'm open to guidance from others."
"I always say what I think no matter what."	"I hold my opinion and listen to others."
"I stir up strife and trouble with words."	"I seek to solve problems and act in peace."
"I don't often learn from my mistakes."	"I make corrections when I make mistakes."
"I lose my temper and act in rage and mockery."	"I control my emotions when needed."
"I like gossip and use words to hurt others."	"I don't talk about others behind their backs."

Walk on the wise side and be as clever as a lion. Remember, you were born to roar!

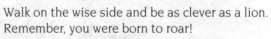

MY ROAR
Look up the following verses in Proverbs: 12:15, 18:2 and 6, 26:11, 29:9 and 11. Can you match each verse to one from the list above?

PONDERING PAWS

Talk to God about the difference between the words "wise" and "foolish."
Look up each one in the dictionary. Journal what you find.
Ask God to tell you where you are acting wisely.

BLIND LEADING THE BLIND

UNDER THE TREE

Brody asked his friend, Casey, if he would teach him to play soccer. Casey said, "I'd love to teach you." But, Casey had never played soccer before, and he didn't know how. Hmm!

Sarah asked her Aunt Kathy to teach her how to knit a stocking cap. Aunt Kathy said, "Of course I will!" But, she didn't know how to knit. Hmm!

Emery invited Erin to the ice-skating rink to go ice-skating. "I'll teach you how to skate on the ice," said Emery. Neither girl had ever put on a pair of ice skates. Hmm!

Kevin and Kyle were at Kyle's grandfather's farm. Kyle found his grandfather's 4-runner key, and the boys decided to go for a drive. Neither boy had ever driven a 4-runner. Hmm!

These are tales of "the blind leading the blind." Jesus warned us about following those who will lead us astray. Luke 6:39 (NLT) says, *Can one blind person lead another? Won't they both fall into a ditch?* Jesus is telling us not to end up in a ditch. He is helping us to use common sense concerning who we are following.

What kind of friends are you learning from and putting your trust in? Lions don't follow just any old lion. They don't go with just anything they see or hear. They are wise! Use common sense because you were born to roar.

MY ROAR

Are you a leader or a follower? If you are a leader, teach someone how to do something you really *know* how to do. If you are a follower, then learn from someone who knows more than you.

PONDERING PAWS

Ask God what He wants to say to you today.
Listen and write what you hear.

TRUTH WILL SET YOU FREE

CHEW ON THIS
Then you will know the truth, and the truth will set you free.
John 8:32 (NIV)

UNDER THE TREE

Kayla had been struggling with fear and insecurity since she was a little girl, but you would never know by watching her actions. Her classmates were fond of her, and she had many friends. She was sweet, smart, and beautiful on the outside, but Kayla hurt inside. The enemy had told her many lies about herself. When Kayla made a mistake, shame and anger boiled inside her. Deep down within her heart, she felt sad and hopeless.

One night when Kayla went to bed, she fell into a deep sleep and began dreaming. Suddenly, she found herself in a jail cell with a big door. A bright white light immediately filled the cell and surrounded her. The cell door opened! The figure of a man filled the space around her. Everything within her wanted to explode. The man standing in front of Kayla looked perfect. He had long brown hair with eyes like white fire. His eyes looked through her as if He knew everything about her. Nothing was hidden from Him. It was Jesus, the Lion of Judah. He was so real to her. He was powerfully fierce but filled with love! Kayla had read all about Jesus in Bible stories, but there He was in her dream and as real as could be. He gently took her hand and led her out of jail and into freedom.

When she awoke, something had changed. Suddenly, she felt empowered by truth about herself. She felt mighty, beautiful, loved, smart, secure, and unashamed. She had met the One who is TRUTH, and He set her free from lies. Ask Jesus to show you who you really are, not who people say you are. It only matters what God thinks. He wants to free you too, because you were born to roar.

MY ROAR

Find a blank piece of paper and a pen or pencil. Make a picture of a jail cell. Write down inside the cell any lies you believe about yourself. Outside the cell, write words that are opposite of those you wrote in the cell.

PONDERING PAWS

Talk to Jesus about how you see yourself. Pour your feelings out to Him.
Let Him remove you from the cell of lies from the enemy.

PRIDE GOES BEFORE A FALL

UNDER THE TREE

Once there were two lions who wandered away from their den. Along their journey, they looked for a cozy place to rest. "Let's go into the forest," said one lion to the other. The lions thought the forest would be full of small, yummy animals to eat. As they headed deep into the nearby forest, they saw there had been a forest fire. Where beautiful tall trees had been, now there were just blackened stumps. At first, the lions cried, "Oh no!" Then they thought a minute. "But, wait! Maybe it's not so bad. At least, we won't have to deal with those pesky hyenas," one lion said to the other. "They won't come into a burnt forest."

The next day a funny little monkey came along. "Why did you sleep here last night? The forest has burned down, and it's not a good place for sleeping," he said. "If the rains come, you will be drowned." With a joint, prideful roar, the lions asked, "Who are you, monkey, to tell us what to do?" They drew their claws at him and scared the monkey away.

Later that very day, a big black cloud of rain appeared over the forest. When it broke open, the rain fell in thick sheets. It rained for many days and nights. There was so much rain that the river swept over its banks. The water covered the burnt stumps, flooding the forest! The lions ran for their lives and within minutes made it to safety. "If only we had listened to the monkey," they cried. The lions' pride and arrogance had led them into great danger.

This lion story tells us what can happen when we enter into pride. The lions wouldn't take good advice from the monkey. Their pride and self-importance kept them from listening. It almost caused them to lose their lives in a flood. Don't allow pride to keep you from making good choices. Don't forget that you were born to roar.

MY ROAR

Look up the word "pride" in a Bible concordance. (It's the dictionary in the back of your Bible.) Find and read three or four scriptures that deal with pride. Next, look the word up in a regular dictionary. Write your results in the *Pondering Paws* journaling section.

PONDERING PAWS

Record your *My Roar* results on your journaling page.
Pray and talk to God about any areas of pride in your life.

PUT YOUR HOUSE IN ORDER

CHEW ON THIS

Put your outdoor work in order and get your fields ready; after that, build your house. *Proverbs* 24:27 (NIV)

UNDER THE TREE

Is your room a mess? Are you a messy or a neat-nik? If you're a messy, then here are some tips on putting your room in order:

- Declutter, pick up, and put away your clothes.
- Start your own laundry in the washing machine.
- Dust all surfaces.
- Wipe the windows and the mirrors with window cleaner.
- Vacuum or dry mop your bedroom floor.

God is attracted to clean rooms. Your heart is like a room for God, so is it messy or clean? The Holy Spirit is attracted to a clean heart. He said to a king in 2 Kings 20:1 (NIV), *Put your house in order*. Putting your house in order means decluttering your heart. Decluttering is clearing away hurts and worries so you can receive Jesus' love.

Let God bleach and launder your heart. Maybe you need to dust off your Bible and read it. Clean up messes made with people you have hurt. Last of all, give your heart 100% to Jesus. Turn from doing what you want to do when you want to do it. That's sin! Ask Jesus to forgive you for going your own way. How clean is the room of your heart? Life's more fun when you have a clean room and a clean heart. You were meant to be free from clutter because you were born to roar!

MY ROAR

Help a friend clean their bedroom. Then tell them how to allow Jesus to clean their heart.

PONDERING PAWS

Is it hard for you to clean your room? Is it hard to set aside time with God each day? Here are some things you can do to make time with God a lot of fun:

- Find worship music you like and listen often.
- Set aside a place and time to be with God and read your Bible.
- Set a timer for 5-10 minutes. Pray until the timer goes off.
- Invite a friend to come over and join you. Use fun pens and colored pencils to underline scriptures in your Bible.

I'M MY BROTHER'S KEEPER

CHEW ON THIS

If we love our brothers and sisters who are believers,
it proves that we have passed from death to life.
1 John 3:14 (NLT)

UNDER THE TREE

Families that play together, stay together. Lions can be fierce toward lions outside of their own family. When it comes to family members, lions are playful and caring toward each other. We greet family members with hugs and kisses. Lions greet their family members by rubbing heads and licking each other. Male lions rub so hard, they knock each other to the ground. Lion cubs even leap upon each other's backs, biting at their necks. But, it's not just for greeting and fun rough play. They are practicing through play for when they grow up and hunt. Lions bravely attack large animals like buffalo or zebra by jumping on their backs.

God designed your family to be a place to have fun and practice love. As you grow, you'll learn to love like Jesus loves. Love says something! It says that mistakes and wrongdoing can be forgiven. Fear and control say, "I'm angry at you and must punish you for what you've done to me." Control withholds love and fun in order to get back at someone who hurts us.

Being your brother's keeper means being lion-like and roaring through hurts and quarrels. Ephesians 2:6 (KJV) says that we *sit together in heavenly places*. That means we have the ability to love on earth as they love in heaven. Being your brother's keeper is learning to practice love because you were born to roar!

MY ROAR

You are your brother's keeper.
Change your attitude toward someone in your family who has hurt you.
Start blessing them and giving them a hug when you greet them.

PONDERING PAWS

Talk to God about someone in your family, or a friend, who has hurt you.
Forgive them and ask God to teach you to love.

NO REST FOR THE WICKED

UNDER THE TREE

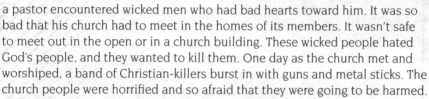

Do you believe God can defend you against wickedness? Wickedness means monstrous, sinful, vile, or evil acts.

Want to hear a lion's story about wickedness? Far away from America, a pastor encountered wicked men who had bad hearts toward him. It was so bad that his church had to meet in the homes of its members. It wasn't safe to meet out in the open or in a church building. These wicked people hated God's people, and they wanted to kill them. One day as the church met and worshiped, a band of Christian-killers burst in with guns and metal sticks. The church people were horrified and so afraid that they were going to be harmed.

The pastor immediately led them in prayer, asking for God's help. God loves His church and hears our prayers. Suddenly, three lions appeared at the door of the home church. The lions began attacking the wicked men. One lion dove upon a man with a gun and dug its teeth into his neck. The bad man was killed instantly. The remaining men ran away in fear. The lions took one long look at the Christians. Then they turned and ran out of the house and back into the forest. It was a miracle! God had sent lions to save His church in a spiritually dark country. The pastor said that they had never seen lions in their part of the land. God had sent the lions to help His people.[8]

This story is a true lion tale about how God can defend us. It is a modern day "Daniel in the Lion's Den" story. God protects those who are His and fights against the wicked. Peace belongs to those who know Jesus as Lord. There is no rest for the wicked because when God's people pray—when we become strong in God—the enemy has to flee. Take your place as one of God's young lions because you were born to roar.

MY ROAR

Use your phone or your parent's phone recorder. Tell your own story of something amazing Jesus has done to help you. Play it back for your family or a friend. Pray for Christians who live in dangerous places around the world.

PONDERING PAWS

Ask God a question and wait for an answer. Write the question under
Pondering Paws. Use a pencil to write the question and a pen to record what
you hear God saying.

MANY ARE CALLED, BUT FEW ARE CHOSEN

CHEW ON THIS
For many are invited, but few are chosen.
Matthew 22:14 (NIV)

UNDER THE TREE

Have you ever been in a contest or tried out for something? There are tryouts for things such as acting, cheerleading, sports, or singing. A tryout is a type of contest or interview to discover someone's capacity to do something. An interview, tryout, or audition takes someone through tests and trials. The purpose is to see who is best qualified to make it to the end. Tryouts are open to anyone at first, but the requirements narrow the field to a smaller number of people. In the end, few make it to the finish line. Few are chosen!

God has His own tryouts that are very different from the world's. He goes after the heart rather than the outward performance. Father God is looking for those who want to become His sons and daughters. His tryouts are about choosing between two roads and picking the right one.

In Matthew 7:13, Jesus tells us that there is a wide path that many people will take. It's the most popular path because it's the easiest, but it also is the sad path that leads away from God and toward darkness. The second path is narrow, and few people take it because it's hard at times. This is the path that Jesus walks. The Jesus path has fewer people, but in the end, it's the best. The Jesus path leads to the Father's porch steps and into His house in heaven. It is the way to eternal life through Jesus.

Right choices lead to happy outcomes; bad choices lead to sad results for us. You can't walk down two paths at the same time. You must choose!

Many are called, but few are chosen because of their own wrong heart choices. God lets anyone and everyone try out for heaven. But, in the end, few get in because they don't choose the Jesus path. Remember, you were meant to walk with Jesus, and you were born to roar.

MY ROAR

Let your roar be in making right choices.
Be the one at the end of the tryouts who has chosen rightly. Choose Jesus today!

PONDERING PAWS

Journal to God about the path you've chosen and why.

ARMED TO THE TEETH

UNDER THE TREE

A young lion was sharpening his big, scissor-like eyeteeth against a tree stump. Another young lion happened to be walking by. The passing lion was always bragging and making fun of other lions. He roared louder than all the other lions, trying to appear fierce. He pranced around the pride acting tough and powerful, watching for the enemy. "Why are you sharpening your teeth?" asked the passing lion. Without skipping a beat, the young lion replied, "When real danger comes, I'll be prepared." The haughty, passing lion shrugged. "When a threat appears, there won't be time for such foolish work as this." But, the lion with the big teeth just kept right on sharpening. The arrogant lion walked away.

Soon, the lazy, prideful lion was met face-to-face with an adult hyena. Because his teeth were dull, he was unable to tear into the enemy's flesh. He was overtaken and eaten! But, the wise lion who had sharpened his teeth was ready. He could face any animal that would come against him.

God wants to help us sharpen our weapons for warfare against the devil. Our weapons are God's Word and confidence in God as Father and caregiver. Stay prayed up, keeping your heart clean of darkness and unforgiveness. These are your weapons, and you were born to roar!

MY ROAR

What are your weapons against the enemy? Make sure you have a good Bible and that you are reading it daily. Use your *Roaring Through the Word* Bible reading guide (found on pg. 203) to help you stay on track.

PONDERING PAWS

Let God check your heart. Journal to God about any hurts or
unforgiveness you may have toward someone.
Choose to forgive and let God heal your hurt today.

_____

_____

_____

_____

_____

_____

_____

_____

_____

_____

_____

_____

_____

_____

_____

_____

_____

_____

_____

_____

MORE BLESSED TO GIVE THAN RECEIVE

UNDER THE TREE

It's more fun to give than to receive. That's a radical thought! Being blessed and receiving blessing isn't magic. It is something from our heart that pleases God. Giving can be an answer to a problem. Here's a Bible story where someone your age had an answer to a problem. See how it can be exciting to solve a problem with a blessing. Here's what can happen:

Jesus was teaching a large crowd on a hill. When it was dinnertime, Jesus asked one of His helpers a question: "Where will we get bread to feed these hungry people?" The man didn't know what to say! He had no money to feed a crowd of people! It would cost a lot—more than six months' wages—to feed them all.

But, a boy, overhearing Jesus and His helpers, popped out of the crowd. "How can I help solve this problem?" he asked. Opening his backpack, he showed them two fish and five loaves of bread. At first, they didn't think it was enough food for so many people. But then Jesus took the loaves and fish, and He thanked God for them. He divided them up among the people, and when the meal was over, they gathered twelve baskets of leftovers.

When a child shared his lunch, it showed something special about kids. Children can have answers to problems when they know Jesus. When there's a problem, you can offer a solution. God's power can work through you. Look around and see how your big heart and faith can make something impossible, possible. There's something you can give to resolve a challenge the world is facing. What ideas do you have to help make your family, school, and city better? You don't have to be an adult to solve a big problem because you were born to roar.

MY ROAR

Look for a challenge that needs a solution. Don't limit yourself! Ask God for an answer to how you can help. Write down the problem and your plan!

PONDERING PAWS

Journal what God is showing you from *My Roar*.

BETWEEN A ROCK AND A HARD PLACE

CHEW ON THIS

When you're in over your head, I'll be there with you. When you're in rough waters, you will not go down. When you're between a rock and a hard place, it won't be a dead end.

Isaiah 43:2 (MSG)

UNDER THE TREE

In the Bible, a shepherd boy named David found himself between a rock and a hard place. This now famous boy learned to roar the hard way. David's dad sent him to check on his brothers in God's army. When he got to where his brothers were, he heard a deep voice mocking God. It was the voice of a giant named Goliath. Hearing someone scoffing and mocking God emboldened David. He didn't have time for fear. He convinced the king to let him fight the giant. Carrying his sling, David gathered five smooth stones. He could hear the almost 10-foot-tall, sword and spear-wielding giant laughing at him.

As David put a rock in his sling, he must have thought, "What have I gotten into?" Surely, he felt he was in over his head. He was between a rock and a hard place, but he couldn't back out now. Pushing through his doubt, he aimed and swung a rock at Goliath's head. The rock hit its mark, and the giant fell backward. Then David picked up Goliath's sword and cut off his head. The evil army turned and ran away upon seeing their giant hero killed. God's army won the battle because of a boy's trust in God!

Have you ever felt you were in over your head, thinking, "I don't know how to do that"? Is there something you don't think you can do? God may be saying, "Yes, you can!" God knows our fear and hesitation when trying something new. Trust Him to help you to press through uncertainty and fear. Pushing through could change something in your life or in the lives of others. David was lion-like because he let God move him beyond a rock and a hard place. You can be courageous too because you were born to roar.

MY ROAR

Do something that seems beyond your natural ability, where you must trust God. Record what happened in your journal.

PONDERING PAWS

Read the story of David and Goliath in 1 Samuel 17:1–51.
Record what happened from *My Roar*.

MAN CAN'T LIVE BY BREAD ALONE (PART 1)

CHEW ON THIS

Jesus answered, "It is written: 'Man shall not live on bread alone, but on every word that comes from the mouth of God.'"

Matthew 4:4 (NIV)

UNDER THE TREE

Have you ever been tricked into doing something wrong? Tricked means to be misled, tempted, fooled, duped, conned, or hoodwinked. The devil's a master trickster who likes making us think right is wrong and wrong is right. He's the father of lies. But, did you know there is a way to become trick-proof against him? God's Word makes us trick-proof. The devil hates the Word of God because God's Word is truth. In fact, quoting the Bible makes him run away. To be lion-like, we must know how to use the Bible against him. Jesus was lion-like and shut the mouth of the devil with God's Word.

When Jesus was baptized by His cousin John, something amazing happened to Him. He came up out of the water and the Holy Spirit tapped His shoulder. Then the voice of God thundered, *This is my Son, whom I love; with him I am well pleased* (Matthew 3:17, NIV). Father God was marking Jesus as a beloved Son. He said, "This is who You are, Jesus, My own Son." At that very moment, Father God affirmed His love for Jesus. He wants to affirm His love for you too.

After Jesus' baptism, He was hanging out with God in the desert. He hadn't eaten anything for 40 days, and He was very hungry. The devil saw His hunger and said to Him, "If You are really God's Son, tell these stones to become bread." But Jesus answered with Scripture, *Man shall not live on bread alone, but on every word that comes from the mouth of God* (Matthew 4:4, NIV).

Next, Satan showed Jesus many kingdoms and their riches. He tried tricking Him into taking the kingdoms for Himself. But, every time the devil tried to trick Jesus, He answered with a Bible verse. Belonging to the Father and knowing His Word empowered Jesus against the devil.

You too can be powerful against the schemes of the devil. Just like Jesus, you can know you are a son or daughter of the King. Use God's Word as a way to trick-proof your life from the devil. Remember, you were born to roar.

MY ROAR

If you have never been baptized, ask God about it. Talk to your pastor or a parent about it. Put Matthew 4:4 on an index card and memorize it. Begin collecting Bible verses and write them on index cards. Punch a hole in the top corner and connect the cards with a metal ring or string.

PONDERING PAWS

Talk to God! Ask, "Who am I to You, God?" Wait and listen for an answer.
God's voice to us is always loving and kind.

MAN CAN'T LIVE BY BREAD ALONE (PART 2)

CHEW ON THIS
Man does not live on bread alone but on every word that comes from the mouth of the LORD. *Deuteronomy* 8:3 (NIV)

UNDER THE TREE

One of the yummiest treats at Disneyland are churros. People wait in line for hours to get a taste of them. Churros are crisp on the outside with soft and tender bread on the inside. Just thinking about them will make your mouth drool! Churros are called the awesome, the lit, and the legit. When you're really hungry, waiting can be tough. The Bible tells us that Jesus knew a lot about being hungry.

Full of the Holy Spirit, Jesus went into the desert to pray. Jesus denied Himself food when getting away to be alone with God. That's called fasting. Fasting is a way to tell God, "I care more about You than about food right now." You can fast TV, movies, and other things for a short time. It tells God you really love Him more than anything. That's what Jesus did in the desert, so He was hungry!

Walking along, Jesus suddenly heard the voice of the devil. "There's no reason to be hungry," he snickered. "If you're God's Son, turn a stone into bread and eat it." That was so uncool and lame of the devil, while Jesus's stomach growled with hunger. But, Jesus loved God more than His daily bread. Jesus knew how to resist the devil's voice. When the devil kept promising Jesus many things, Jesus kept saying NO. He remembered a Bible verse, Deuteronomy 8:3 (NIV), that said, *Man does not live on bread alone but on every word that comes from the mouth of the LORD.*

The devil hates the truth from God's Word. He also hates kids who know they're a son or daughter of God. He is afraid of you when you realize you're loved by God! You can make the devil shake and quake in his boots. Who are you, and whose are you? Do you know? It's Gucci to know God is your Father! That means it's cool! So, never forget who you are because you were born to roar.

MY ROAR

Think of something you like to do. Can you give it up for one week? Can you give up soda, sweets, TV, etc. for one week? That is called fasting for God. It's telling God, "I love you!"

PONDERING PAWS

Spend time with God every day. Let God speak to you while you are doing your weeklong fast. Write what you hear!

SOFT ANSWERS TURN AWAY ANGER

UNDER THE TREE

God built a helpful tool right inside you. It's more powerful than anything you can imagine. It's more powerful than money, brains, or talent. You want to know what it is? It's the power of your voice. Your voice speaking clearly what God puts on your heart is also your roar. There's nothing more exciting than delivering a message God gives you. Saying what you're passionate about can change the atmosphere around you. Your words have great power. They can make sad people happy and angry people calm. Your voice has the power to release God ideas.

Satan does everything he can to keep you from discovering the power within your voice. He will try to keep you from releasing your sound! Your sound can quiet the devil's sound. Proverbs 15:1 tells us that soft answers turn away anger. A soft answer is using your voice God's way. It's responding to cruel, mean, or angry words with calm, mild, gentle, tender words.

God's words act like a sword that can cut off the head of the giants in your life. Giants are those words that overwhelm and hurt the heart. Angry words can also be like a giant at times. It's normal to feel anger, but it's not right to use words to hurt. You may see adults become angry and then wound others with their words. That doesn't make it right.

Learn to share angry feelings rather than hold them in and say harmful things. It's okay to say, "I feel so angry right now!" But, it's not okay to cause others pain with your words. It's not okay to call someone names or lash out physically.

Say you're playing in a sports event, and you lose the game because the referee made a bad call. It's okay to be angry, but tell God how you feel and then move on! Your voice can be a problem or an answer to a problem. Become lion-like in using your words God's way because you were born to roar.

MY ROAR
The next time you feel angry, tell someone, "When you…blah, blah, blah…, it made me feel so angry." Or, "When I saw…blah, blah, blah…, it made me feel so…angry."

PONDERING PAWS

Journal to God about some things in your life that make you really angry.
Ask God to help you process and pinpoint why you are angry.
Talk to Him about it.

_____

_____

_____

_____

_____

_____

_____

_____

_____

_____

_____

_____

_____

_____

_____

_____

_____

_____

_____

A LABOR OF LOVE

UNDER THE TREE

After a long day of hunting, lions regroup and show love by greeting each other. They lick one another and rub their heads against each other. It's one of their love languages. Every boy and girl has a love language from God. It's good to receive love and show love. A "labor," or expression of love, was created by God and is from His nature. God is love! So, God made us to love too. Love is a type of God language or lingo! It's a way God directs His love through us toward others. There are four languages we can use in giving and receiving love. They are: *Cheering Up, Helping With, Time for Others, and High Fiving.* The way you give out love is often the way you feel loved.

A boy named Sean is always happy and wants others to be happy too. He gives away love by cheering up others. One day his father lost his job and was very angry and discouraged. So, Sean decided to write him a letter, telling him what a great dad he is. It made His dad feel so loved.

Twelve-year old Ebony shows love through helping. She often babysits her little brother. Reading him his favorite books and pushing him on the swing satisfies her heart. Helping and caring for others is her language and labor of love.

Sofia loves spending time playing games with friends and family. Time with people is more important to her than cleaning her room. People are more important to her than doing homework or even dance class. She adores being with people, talking and listening. Time for others is her love language and labor of love.

Adron is a hugger! He taught his family to meet and greet each other with a hug. He thumps his friends on the back. He also high fives them when they win or accomplish an important task. Touching is his love language and labor of love. Everyone needs a touch! But, always be powerful, saying "no" anytime someone's touch makes you feel uncomfortable.

Our "labor," or expressions, of love were created and given to us by God. It's another way to become lion-like and express our roar in the world.

MY ROAR

How do you express love to others? Identify your giving love language and act on it with someone. Record what happened in the journaling section.

PONDERING PAWS

Just like you have a giving love language, you also have a receiving one. Talk to God about your personal receiving love language. How do you like to receive love? (*Cheering Up, Helping With, Time for Others and High Fiving*). Tell God you love Him.

THE WRITING'S ON THE WALL

CHEW ON THIS
Suddenly the fingers of a human hand appeared and wrote
on the plaster of the wall, near the lampstand in the royal palace.
Daniel 5:5 (NIV)

UNDER THE TREE

At a friend's party, suppose a hand appears from heaven, and say, a giant finger begins writing something mysterious on the wall. What would you think? That's actually what happened at a king's party in Daniel 5 in the Bible. A finger scratched a riddle on the king's wall: MENE, MENE, TEKEL, UPHARSIN. No one knew what it meant except Daniel. According to Daniel, the message wasn't good news for the king. His days as king would be shortened, and he would lose his kingdom. These events turned into a catchphrase that we still use today when something not so good is certain to happen. When something seems bound to go wrong, we say, "The writing is on the wall." Life can teach us lessons when things don't go our way. God allows us to learn from those things. It's like stories are being written upon the wall of our life.

Allison came home from school crying because a classmate had been mean to her. She was caught off guard because she thought everyone would like her. Her mom told her, "The writing is on the wall, Allison." Her mom was giving her a life-lesson. Not everyone in your life is going to like you or understand you.

Also, "the writing is on the wall" in regard to life being unfair at times. The only thing fair in life is that everyone experiences *unfair* situations. You may be the best player on the team, yet you are passed over by the coach. You may have the best grades but are passed by for an award. Someone cheating may be promoted ahead of you. Unfair treatment is a sad part of life! The writing is on the wall regarding fair treatment.

God sees everything! He doesn't cause bad things to happen to us, and He will never leave us alone without Him. When "the writing's on the wall," don't be downcast or worried. There will always be life events you can't control. God can be trusted in every situation that comes your way. Trust in Jesus because you were born to roar.

MY ROAR
Do you have people in your life who
don't seem to understand you? How do you
respond when the writing is on the wall?

PONDERING PAWS

Read the whole story of Daniel and the writing on the wall in Daniel 5.
Talk to God about something in your life that has felt really unfair,
and write about it in your journal.

GOING THE EXTRA MILE

UNDER THE TREE

Parents are always saying, "Just go the extra mile." What do they mean by that phrase? Going the extra mile is putting your best foot forward and is the opposite of laziness. It's being lion-like in everything God puts in front of you to do. It's roaring through difficult challenges and great opportunities. Going above and beyond what is expected will always produce something good. Going the extra mile may mean hardship, but in the end, it's worth it. Fear of failure keeps us from going higher and pushing forward, so we can't be afraid of failure.

Brave hearts push through failure and don't let it keep them down. Failure doesn't define you; it teaches you something new. Going the extra mile will cause us to fail at times, but no worries—it's worthwhile! You'll always be a winner in God's eyes when you go the extra mile.

Fourteen-year-old Karthik of Texas went the extra mile. He became the 2018 National Spelling Bee champion. He won by spelling the word—koinonia, meaning Christian fellowship. He pushed on to beat out 278 competing state finalists. To get into the spelling bee, he had to go the extra mile and win at his school. Then he had to pay $750 to qualify for the contest. To win a National Spelling Bee requires going the extra mile and pushing yourself beyond your comfort zone. Let God empower you to go the extra mile. Lion-like behavior is a willingness to go beyond what you feel like doing. You can do it because you were born to roar.

MY ROAR
Pick something you will go the extra mile in over the coming months.
Tell a friend or family member your plan.

PONDERING PAWS

Talk to God about areas where you need His help to go the extra mile.

_____

_____

_____

_____

_____

_____

_____

_____

_____

_____

_____

_____

_____

_____

_____

_____

_____

_____

A Fly in the Ointment

Chew on This

Dead flies putrefy the perfumer's ointment, And cause it to give off a foul odor; So does a little folly to one respected for wisdom and honor. *Ecclesiastes* 10:1 (NKJV)

Under the Tree

Paige popped the cap off her Wonder Girl lip balm. The sweet strawberry smell immediately hit her nose. A fly buzzed her head and landed in the center of the balm. There was a fly in her lip balm! Is there "a fly in your ointment?" In other words, is something or someone spoiling a good situation for you? Ointment smells good, and flies make things smell bad. Flies represent something that can ruin a good thing for you.

Let's say ointment represents the fragrance of joy, happiness, faith, safety, and peace. Those are things we're meant to carry within our heart. They are like good-smelling ointments. But, sometimes sad things happen that allow flies into that ointment. In other words, our hearts can be contaminated when hurt comes in.

Flies like to hang around garbage and are attracted to things that smell bad. That's why it's important to get rid of those things in our hearts that attract flies. Forgiveness is the best way to get the fly out of the ointment. Tell someone you trust what you are feeling because keeping hurt inside causes shame. Fear and shame attract flies into our hearts and lives. You'll know if you have flies in the ointment of your heart. Check out this list of "flies":

Fly List

anger, yelling, disobedience, disrespect toward adults, withdrawing, hitting, punching, slamming doors, demanding your way, nightmares, crying a lot, being rude, mean, bullying, bossy, fearful

Even one of these can be a sign of a fly in your ointment. Let God remove these harmful things from your life. The first step is saying you're sorry for acting out your hurt and pain. Next, forgive anyone who has hurt you. Last of all, crawl up on Papa God's lap and let Him love you.

My Roar

If you're experiencing flies in your ointment, let God remove them. Talk to someone, forgive, and let God's love hold you tight.

PONDERING PAWS

Journal and talk to God about anything that has been hurting your heart.

WOLVES IN SHEEP'S CLOTHING

CHEW ON THIS

Watch out for false prophets. They come to you in sheep's clothing, but inwardly they are ferocious wolves. *Matthew* 7:15 (NIV)

UNDER THE TREE

A devious, hungry wolf watched a shepherd caring for his sheep. The wolf thought, "How can I trick the shepherd and his sheep?" Then, one day, the wolf came upon a sheep skin on the ground. He placed the skin on his back and walked unnoticed among the sheep.

One lamb followed the wolf by mistake, thinking he was its mother. Once apart from the others, the wolf turned and tried to eat the lamb. Realizing the wolf wasn't its mother, the lamb ran away. That evening the wolf, still in sheepskin, followed the herd to the barn. He was thinking he might be hungry later. The farmer who owned the sheep became hungry for lamb stew. Aware of the wolf's disguise, he picked him for his stew. The wolf was chopped up and put into the soup pot.[9]

This hungry wolf story shows how evil intentions can have a bad ending. Also, people may look and act good on the outside, but some are wolves on the inside. God doesn't want us to be suspicious of everyone around us. He wants us to be lion-like and discern good from evil. The farmer knew how to pick out the wolf from among the sheep. You can be like the farmer and spot those who might harm you and others. It's hard telling true friends from those who want something from you. Some may seem outgoing toward you, yet they're really out for themselves.

Notice what people say versus how people act. Friends who say they love Jesus but cheat on tests may be wolves. No one is perfect, but we need to learn to recognize evil intent. Stay clear of wolves because you were born to roar.

MY ROAR

Ask God if there is anyone around you who is a wolf in sheep's clothing. Listen and act on what He says. Is there anyone you need to distance yourself from?

PONDERING PAWS

Have you been disappointed when you discovered someone you thought
was a friend wasn't to be trusted? Talk to God about that in your journal.

PART FOUR

MORE ROAR

His Roarsome Voice

Now that you have learned some lion sayings, you are ready to enter into *His Roarsome Voice*. That means God has an awesome voice. Being able to hear God is important to becoming lion-like. Jesus says in John 10:27 (KJV), *My sheep hear my voice,…and they follow me*. Let your ears be open to what and how God wants to speak to you. This part will be a blast! As you practice hearing God's voice and obeying what you hear, you'll roar.

THE TWO DENS

CHEW ON THIS
And God raised us up with Christ and seated us with him in the heavenly realms in Christ Jesus. *Ephesians 2:6 (NIV)*

UNDER THE TREE

Wouldn't it be cool if you could be in two places at once? You can! Earth is our home. Our five physical senses help us navigate life on earth. However, God's heavenly kingdom is also meant to be our home. We are like a lion that lives in two dens—one den high on a hill and the other in a meadow or field.

Jesus had two homes when He walked upon the earth. One was His earthly home where He ate, drank, and slept. His second home was God's heavenly kingdom. We're living on earth too, yet we also have a second home in heaven. Just like seeing, hearing, tasting, smelling, and touching help us act and move in our earthly home, we have spiritual senses that help us when we move and act in our heavenly home. We live and act in both places at once. Here's how!

Your body can be riding a bike while your mind is praying to God. Riding your bike is a physical activity in your earthly home, but praying is using your spiritual senses from your heavenly home. While raking leaves, your heart can be connected to God in prayer. While cleaning your room, you can memorize a scripture. While swimming, you can be hearing God's voice.

That's what it means to be in two places at once. We are seated with God in heavenly places, but living on earth. Ephesians 2:6 (NKJV) reminds us that God *raised us up together, and made us sit together in the heavenly places in Christ Jesus.* Practice living in two dens, and you'll find it's really fun! You were born to roar!

MY ROAR

Can you be in two places at once? Talk to God at the same time you are doing something routine.

PONDERING PAWS

Talk to God about your two homes. Ask Him to show you something
He does when you are in your heavenly home.

_____

_____

_____

_____

_____

_____

_____

_____

_____

_____

_____

_____

_____

_____

_____

_____

_____

_____

_____

_____

BEHIND HIS VOICE

UNDER THE TREE

Did you know there's NO mystery to hearing God's voice? God gives us ways to look beyond His voice to the language He speaks. In the popular TV talent show, "Behind the Voice," people sing a song in different ways. In a similar way, lions use different calls when talking with each other: meows, roars, grunts, moans, growls, snarls, purrs, hums, puffs, and woofs. Each sound has a different meaning. The most famous of these calls is the roar. It is one of the loudest calls in the animal kingdom and can be heard up to five miles away.

God's voice, like the lion's voice, comes in many forms. The most famous and loudest way God speaks is though His written Word, the Bible. Know the Bible, and you will be on your way to knowing how God speaks.

God wants to tell you about Himself through a book He has written for you. That book is not just any book, but God's Word given to us by His Holy Spirit. When we read God's Word, we are hearing God's Bible voice. It can bring us face-to-face with His mind, will, and thoughts. Do you know of any other book that has a voice? God speaks to us through what has been written in His book. Read it and you will hear His "roarsome" voice. In this section, you will learn many ways to hear God's voice. It's so exciting and fun to hear God. He created you to see, hear, touch, and feel His presence. You can come and learn from Him personally. Don't forget...you were born to roar.

MY ROAR

God is love and speaks in a loving, encouraging way. Find a picture of a friend, family member, or yourself. Ask the Lord, "Which Bible character is this person most like?" Listen for an answer. Tell that person what God said.

PONDERING PAWS

Let's do it! Hear God through His Word. Read 1 Kings 19:11–12 (NIV) below.
What is God saying to you about Himself in these verses?

*The LORD said, "Go out and stand on the mountain in the presence of the LORD,
for the LORD is about to pass by." Then a great and powerful wind tore the mountains
apart and shattered the rocks before the LORD, but the LORD was not in the wind.
After the wind there was an earthquake, but the LORD was not in the earthquake.
After the earthquake came a fire, but the LORD was not in the fire.
And after the fire came a gentle whisper.*

SWIVEL EARS

UNDER THE TREE

Remember what you have already learned about the lion's ears? A lion's ears swivel and rotate toward a sound. Facing one direction, the lion can hear from another direction. That's the way God hears us too. No matter where we are, His ears are turned in our direction. God can and does speak to us anytime, but we won't recognize and hear Him unless we're focused and turned toward Him.

Our heart has to act like ears in order to hear God. We have to be turned toward Him, with our spirit facing Him. What is our spirit? Think of your heart like a satellite dish on top of a house. If the dish is facing the right direction, it picks up sound waves in the air. That's what puts the picture on the TV screen. It's like that with hearing God's voice. When turned toward Him, your heart will pick up what He is saying. If the satellite is facing a wall, it won't pick up sound waves. In the same way, we need to make sure obstacles in our lives are removed. Until our heart is pointed upward, we won't know He's speaking.

Think of it like a radio wave that comes into your car. You turn on the radio and tune into the right channel, but you have to be in the car in order to receive the sound. So it is with us. We have to tune into God to hear. Start tuning in today! You will enjoy hearing from your Father in heaven. His voice sounds…soft as a feather. It's as gentle as a dove and as loving as a kind Father.

MY ROAR

Explain to a friend how to hear God's voice using the radio or satellite examples. Practice turning your ears toward God. Ask God simple questions about Himself: what's Your favorite number, color—anything you want to know. Wait and listen until you receive an answer.

PONDERING PAWS

Ask God what His favorite color is and why. Journal what you hear.
Use that color to decorate your journal page today.

SPIRIT TO SPIRIT

CHEW ON THIS

Call to me and I will answer you and tell you great and unsearchable things you do not know. Jeremiah 33:3 (NIV)

UNDER THE TREE

Wouldn't it be strange if your friends never spoke to you? Say you are hanging out with your buddies. What if they never said a word? What if you did all the talking and your friends never talked back? That is called a one-sided connection. We weren't created to have a one-sided relationship with friends, family, and others! God doesn't want that! God wants to speak to us, and He wants to answer when we ask Him questions and talk to Him.

God says that if we call He will answer. Listen for God to speak in a voice that is soft, gentle, loving, kind, calm, and sometimes firm. God's voice isn't mean, confusing, frightening, harsh, shaming, or unkind. His voice doesn't force us to be in a hurry.

Just as you speak your language, God uses a special language to speak to you. His language is placed into your language. Africans hear God in their language. Japanese hear God in Japanese. Germans hear God in German, etc. But, God's language also comes to us through our five senses. Every tribe and people hear God through seeing, hearing, touching, smelling, and tasting. His special heavenly language is poems, rhymes, symbols, and pictures. His language passes to us Spirit to spirit.

You see…God is Spirit, so His breath is spirit. When He breathed life into Adam, a spirit went into Adam. When we come to know Jesus, that spirit we were born with comes alive. God who is Spirit connects with our now alive spirit. That's how we are able to hear His voice. It is Spirit to spirit! Yea! It's so fun to know God and walk with Him. Come and learn the sound of His "roarsome" voice. You were born to roar.

MY ROAR

Practice having a two-sided connection with God. Talk to God from bed tonight. Chat with Him as you do a friend. Stop and wait for Him to answer. Practice hearing Him every night for one week.

PONDERING PAWS

Journal about your *My Roar* experience. Keep your journal
with you in bed. Write down your chat with God.

NONSTOP ROAR

UNDER THE TREE

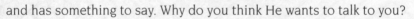

God is a talking, roaring God! Did you know He is talking all the time? In Genesis 1, He even spoke all of creation into being. He is always available to us and has something to say. Why do you think He wants to talk to you?

Why should God speak to ME? It's because He is love. A parent doesn't just write "I love you" on paper and then hand it to their child. Parents say "I love you" in many ways. They show they love you by caring for you all the time. God's voice is like that. God has many ways of speaking to you because He loves you. You will learn how to hear Him as you continue to read through this section of the book.

Another reason God wants to speak to you is to give you good things. The good things are found as He shows you who He is. He wants you to see what He's like. The more we know what He's like, the more we will recognize His voice. We want to be able to hear His voice above other voices. Lions recognize each other's roar. We can know God's voice, which gives us the power to roar for Him.

MY ROAR

Gather four friends and play a one-word listening game. Sit in a circle. Go around the circle, one person at a time. Stop and listen. Ask God for one word to describe each person.
Example: love, friendship, helpful, etc.
Keep going around the circle until each person has four words to describe them.
Try to put the words into a sentence. Fun!

PONDERING PAWS

Get rid of clutter in your mind. Tell God about any known worry or fear. Wait and listen to what God has to say!

GOD'S VOICE THUNDERS

CHEW ON THIS

God's voice thunders in marvelous ways; he does great things beyond our understanding. *Job 37:5 (NIV)*

UNDER THE TREE

Are you afraid of storms? Big claps of thunder sound like a terrifying roar. Thunder can shake a house and your heart to the core. God's voice has many sounds, and one of them is like thunder. We don't need to be afraid of the thundering voice of God. There's something inside the thunder that is meant to inspire, encourage, and help you. Here are five examples of what's hidden inside God's thunderous voice:

- **Belief in Him** – An audible sound startled the crowd standing near Jesus. *Then a voice spoke from heaven, saying, "I have already brought glory to my name, and I will do so again"* (John 12:28, NLT). Some thought it was only thunder. Others thought an angel was speaking. But, Jesus told them, *The voice was for your benefit, not mine* (John 12:30, NLT). His voice thunders to help us believe in Jesus and know Father God.

- **Come** – Revelation 6:1. This verse announces Jesus' return on a white horse ready to conquer. It is telling us to come and conquer too. We are to do those things that bring God's heavenly kingdom down to earth.

- **Worship** – Revelation 14:2. This verse talks about a sound of music mixed in with the sound of thunder. John could hear the people in heaven worshiping God. God wants us to worship Him in spirit and truth. Find worship music you love and play it often. Worship is warfare that fights the devil. The devil runs from worship, but the Holy Spirit and Jesus run to it! They love it when we worship Father God.

- **Prayer** – *The smoke of the incense, together with the prayers of God's people, went up before God from the angel's hand. Then the angel took the censer, filled it with fire from the altar, and hurled it on the earth; and there came peals of thunder, rumblings, flashes of lightning and an earthquake* (Revelation 8:4–5, NIV). Our prayers go up to heaven and then are sent back down to earth. Prayer releases the mighty power of the Word of the Lord.

- **Who Am I?** – *James son of Zebedee and his brother John (to them he gave the name Boanerges, which means "sons of thunder")* (Mark 3:17, NIV). That means they are God's passionate ones. Their lives model the boldness of a lion. God's voice carries our destiny and who God made us to be.

MY ROAR

Take personal action on one of the five thunders of God's voice listed above. Tell someone what you did.

PONDERING PAWS

Pray about the five thunders of God's voice. Ask God to thunder in your life. What do you hear Him say? Journal what you are hearing.

_____

_____

_____

_____

_____

_____

_____

_____

_____

_____

_____

_____

_____

_____

_____

_____

_____

_____

_____

_____

THE SOFT ROAR

CHEW ON THIS

For those who are led by the Spirit of God are the children of God.

Romans 8:14 (NIV)

UNDER THE TREE

Jeremiah 25:38 (NLV) says, [God] *has left His hiding place like a lion.* God and Jesus are lion-like in many ways, but God is still available to you. God listens, and He also speaks.

You use your loud voice when you play outside and your soft voice when you are inside. When God speaks to us, it's like the inside voice. His voice is like a soft roar. If you aren't paying attention, you could miss it. His voice comes as soft as a pillow impression. It's like a butterfly or dove landing on your shoulder. His voice can come like a soft feeling, "I should do…, or my heart feels drawn to…, or I have an overwhelming feeling about…."

Lions have instincts and impulses to act a certain way. God's voice comes to us like that at times.

Recognizing God's voice requires knowing how He likes to speak. His voice never sounds hurried or pressured. God's directions and ideas are clear and peaceful. His voice feels right!

The enemy's voice is the opposite—making us feel pushed and pulled. The enemy's voice will bring fear and confusion. God's soft roar brings peace to the heart. God's voice leaves us feeling like He has wrapped a blanket around our heart.

God's soft roar tells us He is real. Can you hear God's voice? You were born to hear His voice because you're born to roar.

MY ROAR

See if you can sense God's voice speaking to you. "As I talk to God, I have been feeling strongly like I

_____

_____

_____"

PONDERING PAWS

Talk to God about one or two things
He has been impressing upon your heart.

LION-LIKE HEARING (PART 1)

CHEW ON THIS

But blessed are your eyes because they see,
and your ears because they hear. *Matthew 13:16 (NIV)*

UNDER THE TREE

What we think we hear can be comical at times. For example:

You: "How was work today, Dad?"

Dad: "Pretty busy—lots of meetings and deadlines."

You: "You had DEAD LIONS?"

How we interpret what we hear can be really amusing. For example, steak fries. If you didn't know any different, you might think steak fries were made from beef. You might think firing someone from a job means to set them on fire. What if a friend said, "They pulled the wool over my eyes?" You might picture someone with a woolly sheep on their head!

Trust and believe that God wants to talk to you in unique ways. John 10:27 (NKJV) tells us, *My sheep hear My voice...and they follow Me.* God can talk to us anywhere, even when we're busy doing something. But, when you're first learning to hear, quiet listening is best. Try reading God's Word back to Him. That stirs His heart and voice. His Word always gives Him something to talk about with you. The Bible tells us that God is the living WORD. That means He's filled with things to say to you. So, reading His Word, the Bible, helps you to hear His voice.

Jesus didn't just die on the cross for your sins. He died in order to hang out and connect with you. God has a special language He uses to talk to us. Here are some tips on picking up His language. Listen for these clues that tell you He's speaking to you:

- Thoughts and ideas come to you for creating something new—an idea for inventing something or maybe an idea for a school project.
- Someone's name just pops into your head, and you can't stop thinking about that person. Maybe God wants you to help that person in some way or pray for them.
- You receive a strong negative or positive feeling about something or someone.
- A strong impression in your heart is leading you to go this way or that way.
- A Bible verse pops into your head at an odd time. Maybe you're supposed to share that verse with someone or study it for yourself.
- A picture comes to your mind, like on a movie screen.

These are examples of lion-like hearing. God wants to speak to us because He loves us and others. You were meant to hear God's voice, and you were born to roar.

MY ROAR

Place your hand over your heart and say, "God, I am open to hearing You and only You. I silence any voices except Yours. I align my heart, mind, and emotions with the voice of God and Jesus through the Holy Spirit." Practice hearing God's voice from one of the examples above.

Pondering Paws

Say, "Father, I am open to hearing You however you wish to speak to me today." Wait and journal what He is telling you.
Which clue from the list above is He using to speak to you today?

LION-LIKE HEARING (PART 2)

UNDER THE TREE

One night, 10-year-old Katie enjoyed a burger with her family at a local restaurant. Katie's eyes wandered around the room at every bite. Suddenly, her eyes locked onto a little boy across the room, eating with his parents. A thought came to her mind: "They are sad!" Then, another thought came to her mind: "I love them!" Katie had heard these kinds of thoughts before. Listening and hearing God's voice was normal for her.

The more God became her friend, the more Katie heard Him talk to her. She had learned the sound of God's voice. Katie also knew that His voice always agrees with His words in the Bible. His voice always lines up with His nature and character. This was one of those times when His voice lined up with His loving kindness.

So, what should Katie do? What about the boy across the room? Well, she immediately told her parents what she felt God saying. They agreed that God was speaking to her. They walked over and asked the family if they needed prayer. Wow! The family was so happy! They, indeed, needed much prayer because their younger child, the boy's little sister, was in the hospital with cancer. Katie got to be a part of God's plan to help and comfort a hurting family.

God wants us to listen for His voice and be ready to roar at any time. You can help many people by just listening for God's voice and obeying. Listen at school, play, dance, sports, etc. It is as simple as hearing helpful thoughts coming into your mind. That's lion-like hearing! You can be a lion-like listener because you were born to roar.

MY ROAR

Play the family blessing game. Ask God how He wants to speak blessing over each of your family members. Wait and listen! See how God wants to speak something encouraging to you about each family member. Then tell them what He said. You can make a picture or just write them a note.

PONDERING PAWS

Ask God a question. Stop, wait, and listen for a response. Then record what you hear in your journal. Here are three questions you can ask Him:

1) What's Your favorite color in the rainbow?

2) What are Your favorite kinds of prayers to receive?

3) What makes You sad and hurts Your heart, God?

SAY IT FORWARD

UNDER THE TREE

Jesus is the one who designed God's Church. The Church isn't a building! It is people who come together in God's kingdom to love Jesus. Jesus wants His Church to learn love and encouragement, and to speak God's calling and purpose into the lives of others. He tells us in 1 Corinthians 14:3 how to do that. We can hear God's voice in order to strengthen, encourage, and comfort others. When building a house, the foundation goes in first to strengthen the building. Then, like encouraging words build up a person, walls are placed in a house to build up from the foundation. Last of all, furniture goes inside the house for comfort. That's what it means in 1 Corinthians to hear God's voice for others (prophesy).

God is a builder and life giver! Prophesying over others is His way of paying it forward, revealing His message of love toward people. "Pay it forward" is when someone does something for you. Instead of paying that person back directly, you pass something good on to another person. Jesus wants us to "say it forward," instead of pay it forward.

The Say It Forward Game: This is how saying it forward works.

1) God speaks His love to me.
2) God tells me something encouraging that He wants to say to someone.
3) I tell them.
4) They feel loved by God.
5) They hear God say something amazing about someone they know.
6) They tell the person.
7) That person feels loved by God, and it keeps going.

Say it forward is a roar, and you were born to roar!

MY ROAR

Play the Say It Forward Game.
When you say it forward according to
1 Corinthians 14:3, that is called prophecy.

PONDERING PAWS

Ask God to build His house inside you—to strengthen, build up, and comfort you. What did you hear and how does it make you feel?

JESUS IN THE DEN

CHEW ON THIS

And this is my prayer: that your love may abound more and more in knowledge and depth of insight.

Philippians 1:9 (NIV)

UNDER THE TREE

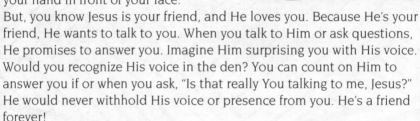

Imagine this, young lions: Your heart and mind is a lion's den or cave. Pretend your friend Jesus is with you inside that den. The den is so dark that you can't see Him. You can't even see your hand in front of your face.

But, you know Jesus is your friend, and He loves you. Because He's your friend, He wants to talk to you. When you talk to Him or ask questions, He promises to answer you. Imagine Him surprising you with His voice. Would you recognize His voice in the den? You can count on Him to answer you if or when you ask, "Is that really You talking to me, Jesus?" He would never withhold His voice or presence from you. He's a friend forever!

What if three bullying lions are prowling around outside of the den? Every time you try to talk to Jesus, these three bullying lions interrupt you. Their voices try to confuse you. They want you to mistake their voices for Jesus' voice. The bullies say things that sound like your friend Jesus. You aren't sure, so you ask, "Jesus, is that You?" Jesus replies, "No, that is not Me!" Be bold and ask Jesus when you are not sure about the voice you are hearing.

Jesus keeps His friends from being cheated out of His voice. You may not see Him, but He is there waiting to talk to you. Jesus' voice was meant to be in the den of your heart and mind. You were meant to hear His voice, and you were born to roar.

MY ROAR

When you are unsure about a thought or idea that comes to your mind, just ask, "Jesus, is that You?" Wait for an answer!

PONDERING PAWS

Who are the bullying voices in your life, trying to interrupt and push out God's voice? Talk to God about them.

_____

_____

_____

_____

_____

_____

_____

_____

_____

_____

_____

_____

_____

_____

_____

_____

_____

_____

THE RIGHT ROAR

CHEW ON THIS

Dear friends, do not believe everyone who claims to speak by the Spirit.
You must test them to see if the spirit they have comes from God.
For there are many false prophets in the world. 1 John 4:1 (NLT)

UNDER THE TREE

"Is it really You, God?" How do you know if it's God's roar speaking through you? There is a battle for the roar that will come out of you. Learn to recognize the three voices that battle each other for attention: God's roar, your own roar, and the devil's roar. You're born to roar with the heart of God in everything you say and do. We can learn to silence all other roars surrounding us. So, how do you know which roar is commanding you? Here are some helps on how to know God's roar.

God's Roar – Things you do and say fit the person you are. God is no different. He will never speak in a way that goes against who He is. Know God's qualities, so you can know when He is speaking to you. God's voice is loving, kind, patient, and caring. He is holy, honest, and pure. He will never speak in an evil way about you or others. God is life-giving, bringing truth and light. What He says agrees with His Word. When God is near, there is a peaceful "yes" feeling inside of you.

My Own Roar – God will put dreams and desires within your heart, but sometimes selfish needs and wants can get in the way. Self-roar is hearing your own thoughts, ideas, and plans without inviting God in. When talking with God, pray and ask Him to remove self from hearing Him. When you feel like you *have to have* an object or your own way, it's your roar. Pray this way:

> "In Jesus' name, I cast out every thought that is not of You. I submit my heart and mind to the Holy Spirit. God, I submit to what You desire for me."

The Devil's Roar – 1 Peter 5:8 (NIV) says, *Be alert and of sober mind. Your enemy the devil prowls around like a roaring lion looking for someone to devour.* The devil wants to steal your "God Roar." The devil will try to whisper bad things into your ear, like "No one cares about you. You're stupid, ugly, and your life doesn't matter." Satan always lies and feeds on death and darkness. That's the language He knows best. God will help you to recognize and avoid the devil's traps, so pay attention to how you feel around certain people and places. God will give you a heads up when the devil is prowling. You will feel a red light is flashing inside you, saying, "NO."

Learn the voices that want your time and attention because you were born to roar.

MY ROAR

Tell a friend about the three roars. Continue to focus on the God roar and practice hearing God's voice.

PONDERING PAWS

- Dial down (get quiet) and unplug your heart (turn off TV, phones, iPad, etc.).
- Plug your heart into God.
- Invite God to speak to you.
- Wait and listen.

Ask the Holy Spirit what He wants to say to you today. Journal what you hear.

GOD-THOUGHTS

UNDER THE TREE

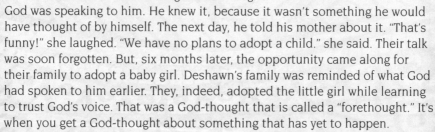

God-thoughts can be big ideas or little ideas, but they are always good and helpful to yourself and others. They come to us inside our hearts or minds.

A 12-year-old boy named Deshawn was lying in bed one night. He couldn't stop thinking of his team's upcoming football game. Out of the blue, a thought popped into his mind, "My family's adopting a child." At first, Deshawn didn't know where the thought came from. Then he heard it again. He waited, and he heard it a third time. He then realized he was hearing a God-thought. God was speaking to him. He knew it, because it wasn't something he would have thought of by himself. The next day, he told his mother about it. "That's funny!" she laughed. "We have no plans to adopt a child." she said. Their talk was soon forgotten. But, six months later, the opportunity came along for their family to adopt a baby girl. Deshawn's family was reminded of what God had spoken to him earlier. They, indeed, adopted the little girl while learning to trust God's voice. That was a God-thought that is called a "forethought." It's when you get a God-thought about something that has yet to happen.

God's Word is filled with stories where He spoke to His people. His written Word gives great encouragement and strength to us, but He also speaks and leads us by His Holy Spirit. He speaks to us today through God-thoughts because He loves us. He wants to tell us what He is doing and about to do. If you pay attention to Him, you'll hear God-thoughts.

MY ROAR

Invite God to give you a God-thought this week.
Ask Him to tell you a scripture He likes.
Stay alert for a God-thought to come to you.

PONDERING PAWS

Ask God to tell you the name of one of His favorite Bible characters.
Write down what you hear. Find two scriptures about that person
and journal what you find out.

_____

_____

_____

_____

_____

_____

_____

_____

_____

_____

_____

_____

_____

_____

_____

_____

_____

_____

_____

_____

_____

IMAGINATION POWER

UNDER THE TREE

God created you with an amazing imagination. Fill in the blank. "If I were a Bible character, I would be _____. If I were an animal, I would be a _____. If I were a vehicle, I would be a _____." Have you ever wanted to fly on the back of an eagle? Have you ever wanted to pet a dinosaur? That's imagination! Did you know that God can use your imagination to talk to you? Imagination is one of your heaven senses, different from your five senses. Your heaven senses kick in when you set yourself apart for God.

Imagination can act like a movie screen in your mind. Imagination is a powerful way God speaks to us. God can even use imagination to show us how He sees us. Creativity is given by our Creator. He made us able to pretend and dream as a way to speak to us.

The devil wants to steal the imagination away from God. He wants to put unclean pictures in the hearts and minds of people. When we give God all our vision, then our images become pure. God is able to tell us stuff through creativity, dreams, or pictures in our mind. Your mind's eyes see what God sees when they are yielded to Him. God wants to speak to you through your imagination so you can roar.

MY ROAR

God can't use your imagination if your mind is cluttered. Too much TV, movies, social media, and video games clutter God-given imagination. Unclutter your mind! Write a note to God, giving Him your imagination. "Dear God, I give You all my creativity and imagination. Please talk to me when I sleep or daydream, in pictures, and more."

PONDERING PAWS

Sit alone with God. Invite Him to fill your mind and imagination with His power and presence. Invite Him to show you what He sees. Make a picture or write down what He shows to you. Begin recording daydreams, night dreams, and pictures He shows you. Ask Him to tell you what they mean.

A LION'S NOSE

CHEW ON THIS

Pleasing is the fragrance of your perfumes;
your name is like perfume poured out.

Song of Solomon 1:3 (NIV)

UNDER THE TREE

Watch the lions at the zoo! Their nose twists and turns with every well-developed sniff. Lions can easily smell prey and guess how long it's been nearby. What about humans? We can smell over 10,000 odors. Did you know our ancestors once used smell to spot disease? They used it to sniff out rotten meat, poison plants, and other food.[10] Have any of your friends taken their shoes off at the movies? Stinky, foul, disgusting, and rank. Bad foot smell is the worst!

We can smell things that can't be seen. Have you heard the phrase, "Something smells fishy to me?" Once on a fishing and camping trip, our car filled with a foul smell. We couldn't see where it was coming from, but it made us want to gag. Looking under one of the seats, we found a fishing bag filled with rotten fish. Your spiritual sense of smell is like that. You can smell something you can't see.

How would you like to smell the fragrances of heaven? They are smells you can't see. God gives us smells from heaven to show and tell us something. For example, the smell of flowers, smoke, and perfumes can be our heavenly investigators. Flower smells may tell us that Jesus is standing nearby. Some scholars believe the Bible is talking about Jesus in Song of Solomon 2:1 (NIV): *I am a rose of Sharon, a lily of the valleys.* The smell of smoke may mean that God is burning away sin in our life. Leviticus 1:9 (NKJV) says, *The priest shall burn all on the altar as a burnt sacrifice, an offering made by fire, a sweet aroma to the* LORD. Ask God for the scents of heaven and let God reveal Himself through smell. You were born to discover the scents of heaven and born to roar.

MY ROAR

Smelling something without a source may be God speaking to you. Pay attention to what you smell near people. God can use smell to help you sense good or evil.

PONDERING PAWS

Write a prayer asking God to let you smell a heavenly fragrance.
Pray God will open up your heavenly sense of smell.
Most of all, pray you can smell His presence.

WORD CARNIVORES

CHEW ON THIS

Consequently, faith comes from hearing the message, and the message is heard through the word about Christ. *Romans* 10:17 (NIV)

UNDER THE TREE

Eleven-year-old Darnell didn't like reading his Bible, so his aunty downloaded a fun Bible app onto his iPad and phone. Darnell was then able to listen to the Bible being read to him. Every night, Darnell went to sleep listening to his Bible app. Then, one day at school Darnell was surprised by the voice of God. A girl named Althea unexpectedly appeared across the table from him in the lunchroom. She was known as the shyest, most insecure girl in the fifth grade. Her curly black hair hung over her face, covering her eyes. She often looked downward, rather than into your eyes when she spoke. Darnell's first impulse was to pick up his lunch and move to another table. Before he could adjust, a scripture popped into his head and stuck there: Joshua 1:9 (NIV), *Have I not commanded you? Be strong and courageous. Do not be afraid; do not be discouraged, for the* LORD *your God will be with you wherever you go.* The verse rolled off Darnell's tongue before he knew what happened. Althea looked up and pushed her hair away from her eyes. Tears could be seen raining down. You see, God used His Word to speak to someone who needed encouragement. He can use you to roar when His words are carried with you.

The lion is called a carnivore because it primarily eats meat. Meat fills the stomach, providing calories and energy for strength and survival. That's what the Word of God does for us. It fills us with strength to survive in times of sadness and also brings us joy. It's like a food source to help us believe, and believing draws us closer to God. Drawing closer to God helps us recognize His voice over others'. That's what happened to Darnell. He filled his lunch sack with God's Word to share with others! You're carrying encouraging words for others when you pack God's Word in your heart.

MY ROAR

First, make a decision to read or hear God's Word. Here are three scriptures that help and encourage others. Memorize all three; then be alert. Share one of them with someone. Record in *Pondering Paws* what happened:

Ephesians 6:10 (NIV) – *Finally, be strong in the Lord and in his mighty power.*

Isaiah 54:4 (NIV) – *Do not be afraid; you will not be put to shame.*

Psalm 56:3 (NIV) – *When I am afraid, I put my trust in you.*

PONDERING PAWS

The verses in *My Roar* are for you to take for yourself.
Let God speak to you through one of the three. What is He saying?

LIONS ON THE RUG
(RECEIVE, UNDERSTAND, AND GO)

CHEW ON THIS
I have called you friends, for everything that I learned
from my Father I have made known to you.
John 15:15 (NIV)

UNDER THE TREE

Do you have a favorite fluffy rug to lay on? Do you have a soft rug to do homework on or just rest on? God gave us a RUG to rest on in hearing and releasing God's voice. As He tells us something encouraging to say to others, we sit upon His RUG. We can use the word RUG to help us make sense of what God's saying.

Visiting a different country without knowing the language can be a problem. That's when we need an interpreter to explain what's being said between people. When God speaks, we need a way to help us make sense of it.

This is how the **RUG** works: **R**eceive>**U**nderstand>**G**o

• **Receive** - The picture, thought, scripture, or words God is saying. It's the who, what, or where of what God wants to say or show you. He may be speaking to you about yourself or giving you a message for a friend.

• **Understand** - What does the who, what, or where mean? It's the explanation of what God is showing you. What does your thought or impression mean? It's the where and how of the word God is speaking to you. We receive what and how God is speaking; then we ask God to explain it.

• **Go** - We say what we receive and understand from God. It's saying what God wants to happen. It's saying what action should be taken based on what God said. Be lion-like, lying upon the RUG of God's voice because you were born to roar.

MY ROAR

Let God speak a happy word to you toward a family member using RUG (*Receive, Understand, and Go*). Practice sitting on it in order to discern and deliver God's words.

PONDERING PAWS

Journal what happened in *My Roar*.
Keep practicing RUG. You can always use your journal entry
to ask God an important question.

TASTING JESUS

UNDER THE TREE

What do you taste like? That may sound funny! It's rare, but some people are born with tangled senses. Tangled senses link what is seen in your brain with different flavors. So, you would have a sense of taste for those around you.[11] What flavor do you think you would be?

Have you ever heard the phrase, "I have lost my taste for…"? Taste can be a liking for or interest in something. What about "that left a bad taste in my mouth?" Taste can be our ability to discern what is good or what is evil. Have you ever been somewhere or with someone and had a bad feeling about it? Practice using your heavenly senses, and you'll be able to taste good from evil. The bad taste in your mouth could mean you are discerning right from wrong.

The Bible tells us that the Lord's presence carries a taste that is sweet. Psalm 34:8 (NIV) says, *Taste and see that the* LORD *is good.* It's so…awesome!

We can't see Jesus in the flesh, but we can smell and taste His presence. The flavor of something is the most important character about it. So, the flavor of Jesus is going to be about His character: goodness, kindness, love, freedom, life, etc. You can taste when Jesus is nearby. His presence always brings something satisfying and peaceful. You can also taste when He is not nearby. That would leave a taste of confusion, fear, and a knot in your stomach.

God's Word carries a sweet, fine taste. Thinking over Bible verses is sure to leave you full and satisfied with your life. God allows us to taste Him, Jesus, and the Holy Spirit when we read His Word. One taste of the true Jesus will fill up your heart. It's not do's and don'ts that fill you; it's tasting Jesus. You were born to taste Jesus and His Word. You were also born to roar.

MY ROAR
Watch for the taste of Jesus in your daily encounters with people and places. What are you tasting? Practice using your heavenly senses everywhere you go.

PONDERING PAWS

Activate the taste of Jesus by memorizing Psalm 119:103.
Give it a try…and let God fill and satisfy you with His Word.
Journal what you think the flavor of heaven could be like.

THE FIGHT FOR PROMISE

CHEW ON THIS

What I am telling you to do agrees with the prophecies that were told about you in the past. I want you to remember those prophecies and fight the good fight of faith. 1 Timothy 1:18 (ERV)

UNDER THE TREE

The best things are worth waiting for. We wait for Christmas to come around every twelve months. Birthday celebrations are also once a year! Things like driving, school parties, and voting are in the future. God's words can sometimes be like that too. God can tell us something good that's going to happen, but we don't see it happening right away. Sometimes we have to fight by prayer for God's words to come to pass. Agreeing with God's words spoken over us can help those words come to pass too.

There is a famous young singer named J.B. When he was born, God spoke to his mom about him. "One day J.B. will help give the music world back to Me," God said. But, for many years, that didn't happen. J.B. went away from God and did many sad things, until one day something changed! He remembered all the things be learned about God while growing up. He remembered the "Catch the Fire" events he attended at church. J.B. is still famous today, and God is using him in a mighty way. Without compromise, J.B. now boldly shares at mega concerts about Jesus. He is a sign of what God wants to accomplish through people.

You see, J.B.'s mom believed God's words over her son. She prayed that God's words would come to pass and they did. You can fight for yourself just as this mom fought for her son. What promises have you heard about your life? Was anything spoken over you as a baby? For example, do you have a heart like a pastor? Then start helping friends with their problems. Maybe God says you are a worshiper like David. Ask how you can get involved with the worship team at church or start a children's worship team. Begin praying for God to bring those promises to pass. Believe what He says and pray for Him to bring it about His way.

MY ROAR

Has God given you a verse, declaration, or promise about your life? Ask your parent about your baby dedication or baptism. Was anything special spoken over you at that time? Start stepping out! Do something now that is related to what God has said about you.

Pondering Paws

Use colored pencils or pens to create a prayer. Talk to God about your future, writing what you hear. Begin drawing shapes around your entry. Make fun doodling shapes until the whole page is filled.

THE COLORS OF GOD

CHEW ON THIS
The one who sat there had the appearance of jasper and ruby. A rainbow that shone like an emerald encircled the throne.
Revelation 4:3 (NIV)

UNDER THE TREE

Lions are color-blind. That means they see light and dark, but not colors. We can be lion-like by walking in God's light. At the same time, we can see what God saw when He created color.

When a friend shows you a picture they created, you might say, "It's so you!" Everything God creates is an expression of who He is too. That's what color in heaven and on earth is. Every color God created is part of who He is and what He loves.

Colors are special to God, and He wants you to know about them. The Bible tells us that there is a rainbow around God's throne: A *rainbow that shone like an emerald encircled the throne* (Revelation 4:3, NIV). There are such beautiful colors in heaven and on earth. God enjoys colors! The colors in the Bible can stand for different things. Here is a list of what some of the colors may mean. Ask your parents if you can use the computer to find even more color meanings online.

Red – The blood of Christ

White – Love of God

Yellow – Eternal life

Violet – God's justice

Orange – Separated from the world and set apart for God

Blue – God's righteousness

Green – Happiness[12]

When praying for someone, God may give you a color impression to encourage them. If that happens, you can turn that color into a prayer. For example, if you see white, "God wants you to know He loves you." For green, "God is happy that you believe in Him and are saved." Learn to recognize the colors in God's heart because you were born to roar!

MY ROAR

What is your favorite color? Can you find a scripture about your favorite color in the Bible? Ask God to give you an impression of a color for a friend. Then tell them what God is saying to them.

PONDERING PAWS

Ask God what His favorite color is.
Journal what you feel you are hearing Him say.
Also, tell God about your favorite color and thank Him for color.

PART FIVE

IMAGINATION DEN

Heaven's Lionized

You're in the final lap to becoming a lion and roaring for Jesus, and you're doing awesome. This last part will stir your imagination and feed your creativity. Let God take your heart to a place you've never been before. Go into the imagination and lionized den. If given to Jesus, your imagination is a doorway into His pictures, ideas, and gifts. Become one of heaven's lionized speakers, authors, painters, or inventors. Lionized means God is applauding you for your actions, creativity, interests, and spiritual gifts. Belonging to God is more than attending church on Sundays. It's carrying His heart into everything you say and do. Part Five will teach you about heaven, angels, and how to bring heaven to earth.

DREAM BIGGER

CHEW ON THIS

Now to him who is able to do immeasurably more than all we ask
or imagine, according to his power that is at work within us,
to him be glory. *Ephesians* 3:20–21 (NIV)

UNDER THE TREE

An 11-year-old boy named Dakota had his own mowing business. God had planted something big inside his heart. Dakota thought it would be good to do something important for God. While mowing his neighbors' lawns, he daydreamed of what he could do one day. The biggest thing he could imagine was to own his own landscaping business. He kept thinking, "I'll have the biggest landscaping office in town one day, so I must mow more lawns than anyone else." Dakota would say to himself, "I can do anything." And his parents would keep telling him, "Nothing is impossible with God."

Fast forward twenty years! Dakota's daydream not only came true, but it was more than he could have imagined. At age 31, he found himself head landscaper for the White House. He now was the caretaker for the president's big yard. He also traveled to different countries, helping governments care for their own presidents' lawns.

God took Dakota's dream far beyond anything he ever could have hoped for. The dream started with his own desire, but God had an even bigger dream for him. Dakota went way beyond his own imagination. What would have happened if Dakota had limited his dreams to just mowing neighborhood lawns? Our heavenly Father will take you beyond what you can dream for yourself too. Learn to dream, and watch God dream even bigger for you. Trust Him to help you to dream big because you were born to roar.

MY ROAR

Trust God with one dream you have for something you want to do right now. Then step out and do it.

PONDERING PAWS

Journal with God about your passions and dreams.
Do you trust God to help you grow and point you toward your dreams?

REIGNING TO ROAR

UNDER THE TREE

How important are you to the world around you? God says that the men, women, and children in His kingdom are very important. There once was a king who was pulled from his throne and tossed into prison. His young son was next in line to be king. The same wicked men kidnapped the king's son and took him far from the kingdom. "We'll raise him to make wrong choices," they said. He would never fulfill the grand destiny the king and God had for him. So, they took him away and showed him many bad things life offered. He was pampered with toys and given many sweets. Anything that made him feel like a slave to the world's ways was given to him. They even used bad words around him and showed him unclean movies. He was exposed to things not suitable for a king.

But, he resisted all the bad that the world had to offer. The boy wouldn't bow to wickedness because he was born for greatness. One day he was set free from his prison. The bad men were punished, and the boy did become king just as planned.

Girls and boys are born to be kings and queens. Many things in this world are attractive and inviting, but when you know you're God's royalty, you'll resist. The way you see yourself results in the way you behave and think. God's truth about us is more important than what people think and say. God loves you through and through. God made you to rule and reign, and we were born to roar.

MY ROAR

Pay attention to what you say, do, and think this week. Are your actions and thoughts the actions of a king or queen? For number 1, write a sentence saying how you feel about yourself. For number 2, write a sentence about how your thoughts and behavior are affected by statement 1.

1._____

_____

2. _____

_____

PONDERING PAWS

What should a child king or queen's day look like?
Journal about those things that make you feel like a king
or queen and those things that don't.

TALKING ABOUT HEAVEN

CHEW ON THIS

After this I looked, and there before me was a door standing open in heaven. And the voice I had first heard speaking to me like a trumpet said, "Come up here, and I will show you."

Revelation 4:1 (NIV)

UNDER THE TREE

Let's talk about heaven! It's a wonderful place, and it's called home to God and Jesus. People die and go there, but they're not ghosts floating on a cloud. They have special new clothes that fit perfectly. The clothes make them look a little different, but mostly the same. In other words, you are still you in heaven. When Jesus went up to heaven after His death, He was still Jesus.

You don't become an angel when you go to heaven. Angels and human beings are totally different from one another. Angels will never become people, and people will never become angels. Angels may look like people at times for God's purpose, but they are not the same. Angels are special messengers, and at times protectors, sent to us from God. (Read Luke 2:9–14.)

God made heaven big enough for all those who are coming in. It's a happy, perfect place of joy and peace. There is no sickness or pain in heaven. It looks a lot like earth, but everything is alive and colorful. That's because Jesus is there with Father God, and they give life. Heaven is filled with worship, and everything growing there worships God. Even the streams and flowers in heaven worship God.

Heaven is a place where people talk to each other and fellowship around God's throne. The best news is that we can have aspects of heaven on earth. Knowing Jesus and following Him brings heaven to earth. Knowing Jesus should make us want to bring to earth what's said and done in heaven. We don't need to be afraid of death because heaven is a wonderful place. For now, your life can bring heaven to earth because you were born to roar.

MY ROAR

Pay attention to what people say about angels and heaven. Test everything you hear with God's Word. God wants you to understand now what heaven is like. Read John 5:24, John 14:6, and Romans 6:23. What do these verses say about who will see heaven?

PONDERING PAWS

Read Revelation 4. Make a list of all the things that are near the throne of God. Does Revelation 4 say anything about a lion?

HEAVEN IS NOW

CHEW ON THIS
Your kingdom come, your will be done, on earth as it is in heaven.
Matthew 6:10 (NIV)

UNDER THE TREE

Have you heard the phrases, "I'm in heaven" or "It's like heaven on earth"? There's some truth to both statements. Heaven is for later, but heaven is also for NOW. The more we see and know Jesus, the more we see heaven. That's because Jesus came to show us what God and heaven are like.

Also, worshiping God brings us closer to Him and closer to heaven. Praying can bring what happens in heaven down to earth. That is part of bringing God's kingdom to earth. Jesus told us to pray for heaven to come down to the earth. Bringing the kingdom to earth is really simple. It's smiling and listening to a friend. It could be helping someone out of a tough spot or hugging someone who's hurting. Saying yes to God— obeying Him—is bringing heaven to earth.

One day an 11-year-old boy named Brett brought heaven to his school playground. A classmate had a broken arm, and it was in a sling. Slings keep broken arms in place so they can heal. Brett felt sorry for the boy because he wasn't able to play and do what others were doing. Brett believed that Jesus could heal the boy's arm. He asked if he could pray for him. The boy said, "Yes." As the teacher and others gathered to watch, Brett prayed a simple prayer of healing. Suddenly, something cracked, and the boy moved his arm. He threw off his sling and began doing push-ups. To everyone's amazement God healed the boy's arm. God's kingdom of heaven had come to earth. You, too, can bring heaven to earth because you were born to roar.

MY ROAR

Heaven is not just for later; it's for now.
How can you bring heaven to earth this week?
Choose something you can do
that brings heaven to earth.

PONDERING PAWS

Talk to God about those things He has empowered you to do to bring heaven to earth. Ask God and journal what He is saying to you today.

HIGH ADVENTURE DREAM

UNDER THE TREE

Eleven-year-old Abby was a high adventure dreamer. Every night she'd lie in bed and thousands of dreams filled her head. But one theme ran through her mind continually—heaven. She loved science and learning about God's creation of the moon, stars, and sky. "What if my surroundings could be MORE like heaven?" she wondered. After she read Psalm 103:19, her heart was captured by God and His home in heaven. One night, her dream seemed so real that she recorded it in her journal:

A bright white light entered my bedroom, and I sat up in bed. A warm breeze blew across my face. I began to fly through space, passing through beautiful, flickering stars. From the starry heavens, I approached a sparkling wall. It was lit with red, yellow, orange, purple, blue, green, and violet. The wall surrounded three giant cities in the sky, one on top of the other. A gate opened, and I entered a magnificent city. Once inside, I was escorted by angels to go and meet someone special. I could feel love coming toward me. I was in awe at the wonderful presence of Jesus. Perfect love that casts out every fear was standing in front of me. My heart felt overcome with thankfulness. I began to sing a worship song I had learned in Sunday school, "Reckless Love" by Cory Asbury. I fell down and worshiped Jesus. Jesus told me to hold out my hand. He placed a gold heart locket in my palm. As I opened the small latch on the locket, a Bible verse appeared inside the heart. It was John 3:16: *For God so loved the world that he gave his one and only Son.*

Then Abby heard her mom's voice, "Time to wake up, sleepy head!"

Some dreams are used by God to show us something. Other times, God uses our dreams to warn us or draw us closer to Him. Dreams can also be silly and have no meaning at all. True God-dreams will cause us to feel peace and joy. Warning dreams will tell us to pray to shift the danger away from us or others. God will speak to us and show us His love whether we're awake or asleep. Remember that you were born to know Him, so you can roar.

MY ROAR
Put on a worship song and spend some time worshiping Jesus. Talk to Him! Share with Him a list of three things you need help with.

PONDERING PAWS

If you have had a recent dream that made you feel closer to God, record it in your journal. The word "heaven" in the Hebrew language spoken in Bible times is *sham-yim*. It means "God's dwelling place." See how many Bible verses you can find about heaven. Read them and write them in your journal.

WAKEY, WAKEY (PART 1)

CHEW ON THIS
For he will command his angels concerning you to guard you in all your ways. *Psalm* 91:11 (NIV)

UNDER THE TREE

The Bible tells us that angels are among us. Did you know that God created different kinds of angels? Some are messengers, some warriors, some helpers, and some healing angels. God's angels stand waiting all around us for their work assignments to be given. They are among us to help bring the kingdom of heaven to earth.

There's a true story of a young girl with a big assignment to awaken one of God's sleeping angels. She was awakened in the middle of the night by a loving presence. A visible cloud appeared in her room—the cloud of God's presence and glory. She pulled the covers up to her chin, waiting for God to speak to her. Suddenly, a strong idea came to mind. The idea was to go to the nearby chapel and yell, "Wakey, Wakey!" She recognized that the impression was from God. He was speaking to her through an idea. The problem was, the idea didn't sound good to her. She didn't want to do something so silly. She said, "I'm sorry God, but I'm not doin' that." Then, the strong feeling came to her again, "Go to the chapel and shout, 'Wakey, Wakey!'" She began to feel that if she didn't do it, she would disappoint God.

Not wanting to let God down, the next day she set out for the chapel. Upon her arrival, she saw many, many people were inside and outside. She was surprised because the chapel was usually empty! Standing on the sidewalk, she tried to gain the courage to speak. A faint whisper came from her lips, "Wakey, Wakey." Under her breath, she whispered, "What will people think of me?" Then God spoke to her heart and said, "Is that how much you want Me here?" Immediately, she felt empowered with boldness. She lifted her head heavenward and shouted at the top of her lungs, "WAKEY, WAKEY!!!"[13]

Would you be so bold? Would you shout nonsensical words in public without knowing what or why? A God idea, impression, or thought is always worth doing. Never be afraid. Working with God brings forth big surprises and something really life changing. Remember, you were born to roar.

MY ROAR

Ask God to open your eyes to see His angels and what they are doing. Never be afraid of God's angels. They are part of heaven and His helpful creation.

PONDERING PAWS

Talk to God about your fears. Ask Him to help you to be bold for Him and to step out. Would you have the courage to do what the girl in the story did?

WAKEY, WAKEY (PART 2)

CHEW ON THIS

As God's co-workers we urge you not to receive God's grace in vain. For he says, "In the time of my favor I heard you, and in the day of salvation I helped you." *2 Corinthians 6:1-2* (NIV)

UNDER THE TREE

What do you think "Wakey, Wakey" means? Why would God tell a young girl to shout such nonsense in public? God chose a child to wake up an important angel and hand out an assignment. God used "Wakey, Wakey" to say "Wake up! Wake up!"

The girl shouted "WAKEY, WAKEY" on the front steps of a packed-out chapel. As she turned to sneak away, the ground under her feet began to shake. Her eyes widened in amazement as a huge angel stepped into view. He was so large that she mostly saw his feet. "What kind of angel is this?" she wondered. "Who are you and what do you want?" she asked. "I'm the angel of fresh love and excitement for Jesus," he said. "I have come to wake up the hearts of people." You see, the angel was there to help bring many more to Jesus and to wake up and refresh God's people. That's called revival![14]

God wants you and me to pay attention and listen for the sounds of heaven. When God speaks, it's fun to hear Him and to step into His purposes. Even a child can partner with God to wake up a sleeping angel. God can wake up an angel in order to wake up a sleeping church.

God's angels are here, and they're among us. We don't pray to or worship angels, nor do we command them. Only God commands them. But, God does not want us to ignore them either. They are here to carry out God's kingdom on earth. They have been sent to assist us, and we need all the help we can get. So, get ready! Angels appear at times when you least expect them because you were born to roar. WAKEY, WAKEY!!

MY ROAR

The Bible mentions angels over 300 times. They are interesting beings, but God wants us to always seek Jesus first. Children often see angels because their hearts are pure before God. They can easily open their God eyes to see what's happening in heaven. That's when God's angels can be seen most easily.

PONDERING PAWS

Read in the Bible about the angels God sends to protect us from harm: Psalm 91:11, Matthew 18:10, and Acts 12:1–18. Ask God what your guardian angel looks like. What is its name? Journal what God tells you.

A FROZEN INVENTION

CHEW ON THIS

He has filled them with skill to do all kinds of work as engravers, designers, embroiderers in blue, purple and scarlet yarn and fine linen, and weavers—all of them skilled workers and designers.

Exodus 35:35 (NIV)

UNDER THE TREE

Being lion-like includes creativity and originality. Lions are resourceful animals with insight and planning. They are artistic in how they hunt and protect themselves and their prides. Even their individual roars are unique and innovative. And you don't have to wait until you're grown up to invent something. You can make the world a better place now. God wants you to dream big! Did you know that a child invented the popsicle?

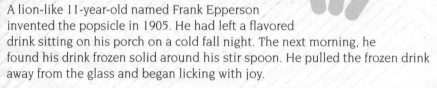

A lion-like 11-year-old named Frank Epperson invented the popsicle in 1905. He had left a flavored drink sitting on his porch on a cold fall night. The next morning, he found his drink frozen solid around his stir spoon. He pulled the frozen drink away from the glass and began licking with joy.

Throughout his childhood, Frank kept thinking about his frozen invention. He served his frozen treat at parties where it was a true winner. The treat was also served at a fireman's ball. Soon he realized it needed to be shared with the world. Different kinds of flavors and sticks were tried until it was just right.

He knew it was a good idea and a God idea, so he applied for a certificate to protect his invention. At first, he decided to call it "Ice on a Stick" and later changed it to the "Epsicle Ice Pop." He sold his ice on a stick for 5 cents each. Then later on, he changed the name again to the "popsicle." In time, the popsicle was sold in grocery stores and ice-cream shops everywhere.[15] What would the world be like without the popsicle? God loves inventions! He wants to give us creative ideas to make the world a better place. You can invent something too because you were born to roar.

MY ROAR

Begin thinking about something useful that needs to be invented. Make a picture of something you think might be a good invention.

PONDERING PAWS

Ask God what He wants to talk with you about today.
Journal what you think you are hearing Him say.

_____

_____

_____

_____

_____

_____

_____

_____

_____

_____

_____

_____

_____

_____

_____

_____

_____

_____

EARMUFF INGENUITY

UNDER THE TREE

Do you need to find a better, easier way to do something? God loves to see His kids think and act creatively to solve problems. Electronics and other items that make our lives more comfortable were invented by someone. Even the earmuffs you wear while sledding were invented back in 1858.

Fifteen-year-old Chester Greenwood lived in the cold state of Maine and loved ice-skating. On a cold winter day, Chester was out testing his new ice skates. The bite of the cold air made his ears sting and throb. Becoming more and more tense, he tried protecting his ears from the cold air. First, he wrapped his head in a scarf, but it was too itchy. The big scarf hindered his view.

He had the idea to bend a piece of wire that fit around his ear. He then recruited his grandmother to sew a round piece of fur inside the wire. It worked beautifully! Over time, he worked to make improvements to his first model. The rest, as they say, is history!

When he grew up, Chester founded the Greenwood's Ear Protector Factory. His company provided ear protectors for U.S. soldiers during World War I. Chester went on to invent many other things. His life is now celebrated in his hometown with a parade each December.[16]

Chester's earmuff ingenuity and clever problem solving helped him become a famous inventor. With the Holy Spirit's guidance and God-given creativity, you can do something amazing. Allow yourself to be used powerfully by God because you were born to roar.

MY ROAR

Being a Christian is more than reading the Bible, praying, and going to church on Sunday. It's being powerful for God in making the world better. Do something, make something, or say something that gives God the attention.

PONDERING PAWS

Ask God to give you some creatively inspired ideas today.
Make a picture of something in your journal or just write what you hear.

TURNING ON THE LIGHTS

CHEW ON THIS

When Jesus spoke again to the people, he said, "I am the light of the world. Whoever follows me will never walk in darkness, but will have the light of life." John 8:12 (NIV)

UNDER THE TREE

Christmas is the best! The celebration of the birth of Jesus is what Christmas is about. The Christmas season helps us welcome Jesus afresh and anew. The Christmas tree reminds us that Jesus brings life into our lives. Draping strings of lights around the tree underscores the light that Jesus brings. Following Jesus is like wearing a string of lights around our hearts. He brings light into the darkness. When we receive Him, we carry His light around with us. You can light up a room with the love of Jesus.[17]

Fifteen-year-old Albert Sadacca made Christmas tree lights popular. Young Albert loved decorating his family's Christmas tree. He was always thinking of ways to make their tree more beautiful. His father owned a store where they sold fake birds that lit up. Albert was fascinated with the beautiful, radiant birds. The light got him thinking...hmm.

Before Christmas 1917, a deadly fire broke out in New York City. It was caused by a candlelit Christmas tree that went up in flames. Hearing of that tragic event gave Albert a God-thought. The lit-up bird in his family store kept coming to his mind. He wondered what a Christmas tree would look like covered in electric lights? "What about selling colored strands of Christmas tree lights at my parent's store?" he thought. It was a great God-idea. Albert's brilliant concept would place a symbol of Jesus in millions of homes. His family loved the idea and put electric strings of lights in their store.

By 1920, Albert and his brothers had created many types of Christmas tree lights. Up until the 1960s, they were the number one sellers of Christmas tree lights.[18] Albert had found a safe way to light up Christmas trees. God wants to give us ideas on how to be world changers too. What about doing something in our home, neighborhood, or school that points people to Jesus? We don't have to be in church to serve Him. The world needs more Alberts, who are born to roar.

MY ROAR

How can you point people to Jesus?
Get an idea and do one small thing that helps point people to Jesus.

PONDERING PAWS

Talk to God today about John 8:12.
Ask God, "What does it mean to be a light?"

IMAGINE HEALING

CHEW ON THIS

Whoever believes in me will do the works I have been doing, and they will do even greater things than these, because I am going to the Father. John 14:12 (NIV)

UNDER THE TREE

Ten-year-old Trinity sat next to her older brother one Sunday at children's church. As she listened to the Bible message, her right ear began to burn. It didn't hurt, but it felt hot! Trinity had learned in Sunday school how to pay attention to her senses. Her teacher had taught the class that God sometimes speaks through our senses. "God is always speaking," she said, so Trinity was paying attention when her ear began to burn. It was like solving a mystery. God wanted her to notice the burning right ear. Then, He wanted her to figure out who might need healing in the ear.

After the service, Trinity asked those around her if anyone had a hurting ear. One junior helper sitting directly in front of her said, "Yes, it's me." He explained how he had fallen through the ice at the age of 8. The accident caused permanent hearing loss in his right ear.

She asked if she could pray for his ear to be healed by Jesus. Then she asked if she could put her hand upon his ear. He said, "Yes, of course!" So, Trinity prayed a simple prayer, "God, heal this ear in Jesus' name." Suddenly, he felt a little pop! He covered his left ear and discovered he could hear in his right ear. Jesus had immediately healed him.

Jesus' disciples healed the sick. The Bible tells us that we, too, can do the things that Jesus did. John 14:12 (NIV) says, *Whoever believes in me will do the works I have been doing, and they will do even greater things than these.* Even young children who believe in Jesus can do what He did in His name. You can heal the sick in Jesus' name. Walking with Jesus and doing what He did is fun and amazing! Put yourself in a Bible story, imagine doing what Jesus did, and do it. You can do what Jesus did because you were born to roar.

MY ROAR

Ask God to place someone in your path who needs healing prayers. Step out and pray a simple healing prayer over them.

PONDERING PAWS

Find a Bible story in the New Testament where Jesus healed the sick.
Imagine yourself in that story line.
Journal how you felt toward the person who needed healing.

_____

_____

_____

_____

_____

_____

_____

_____

_____

_____

_____

_____

_____

_____

_____

_____

_____

_____

HAPPY ANIMALS CLUB™

UNDER THE TREE

Did you know that lions sometimes help and protect other animals? A story recently surfaced about a lioness in Africa who adopted a baby antelope. Other lions tried to attack the lioness protecting the baby. The park rangers protected the lioness as she protected the calf.[19] You, too, can be lion-like and kind to God's animals. Here's a story of a boy who wanted to protect God's animals.

Nine-year-old Jim, a boy in the Philippines, was lion-like. He began feeding hungry, homeless dogs in his neighborhood. Each time he took his own dog for a walk, he came across a stray dog. Jim had the idea to leave food for the dogs outside his house. They were shy at first and only came to eat the food left for them. Bit by bit, they got used to seeing Jim setting out the food for them. Before long, some were coming up to him to be petted and loved on. He rubbed their bellies and combed their fur. The young boy even began bathing them.

His father posted pictures of Jim and his dogs on the internet. Many kind people saw the pictures and loved what he was doing. People began giving him money to feed and care for the animals.

With money coming in, Jim was able to rent outdoor space to keep the animals. His parents helped him every step of the way. Jim had the idea to call his shelter, Happy Animals Club™. This young boy had a lion-like goal, "I want to save as many dogs as I can."[20]

God can give you lion-like ideas to make a difference where you live. Jim was connecting with God's heart in caring for homeless dogs. You can tap into God's heart and do something to change the world around you too. Remember, you were born to roar!

(Note: *Don't ever approach a stray dog unless an adult is with you.*)

MY ROAR

Make a list of something you observe that makes God's heart sad. Ask God if there is something you can do to change it. Always talk to your parents before stepping out.

PONDERING PAWS

Talk to God. Ask Him what He wants to talk to you about today.
Journal what you hear.

THE BULLY BUSTER

UNDER THE TREE

Brandon, age 14, had struggled with suicidal thoughts after being bullied in school. He was different than the other kids. Brandon was a shy kid and found it difficult to put himself out there to be known. His peers bullied him physically and mentally for being different. But, one day, he began to feel more lion-like. He started gathering enough courage to run for class president. His tormentors tore down his campaign signs. They wrote harmful, mean words on them and threw them in school toilets. He didn't have anyone to come to his rescue, but the school had something called a bully box. A bully box is a safe place for students to inform secretly on bullies.

So, Brandon slipped a written complaint into the wall-mounted bully box. In the midst of his ordeal, he paid close attention to the design of the box. He began to wonder how he could improve it. Most of the kids in school had cell phones. He thought, "Maybe I can design a bully prevention tool for the phone." He thought a phone app would be more private and give quick access for reporting.

With his parents' and teachers' help, he started his own software company. Brandon's first product was an anonymous bullying reporting app. That app now is used universally, helping many kids find relief from bullying.[21] Brandon was surrounded by bullies, but became a bully buster. He saw a problem, and he became the answer. Brandon turned a struggle into a software company that helps others.

Lions are strong, brave, and tough against animal bullies, but they learn to fight back and roar to alert other lions of their situation. You can be lion-like and overcome bullying. God promises to never leave us or reject us. Give God your fear like Brandon did and turn it into something helpful.

God can take a bad situation and turn it on its head in a minute. You were born to do great things like Brandon. You can make a difference because you were born to roar.

MY ROAR

Brandon's phone app is: The BullyBox™. Just go to the app store on your cell phone and get it for free. Are you struggling with something? Ask God how you can turn a weakness or struggle into something good. Use the *Pondering Paws* journal section to record what God is saying to you.

PONDERING PAWS

Record what God is telling you to do from *My Roar*.

GENERATION GOOD

UNDER THE TREE

Meet a young lioness, 13-year-old Mercer Henderson. She's the founder of her own company called, 4GirlsTech™. Her company started from her dream to empower girls her age. She loves creating phone apps called Audiots™. The app adds sound to emojis. Many of her friends enjoyed using the emojis in back and forth texting. They also loved sending audio files to one another. So, Mercer thought, "Why not combine the two"? Her parents helped her find an app developer and an expert in sound to pair emojis with a sound.

It took time, but Mercer picked just the right sounds to pair with the emojis. It took her five months to finish the project. Since Audiots™ was launched, she has already seen over 50,000 people use her apps.[22] It takes a lion and lioness with boldness and courage to step out like Mercer.

Girls and guys can be encouraged by her strength and resolve to follow her dream. Good ideas come from our Creator when we're determined to follow Him.

Mercer wants her generation to be called "Generation G," or Generation Good. The name stands for kids her age that make a difference in the world. That's a God-thought because God wants us to bring His kingdom to earth. That means doing acts of goodness and kindness wherever we go.

What if God gave you an idea to create a special Bible app? Pay attention to what is going on around you. Let God invade your thoughts and ideas. Give your imagination to Him. Colossians 3:23 (NIV) says, "*Whatever you do, work at it with all your heart, as working for the Lord.*" God gave us an imagination and ideas to be used for Him and Him alone. We can find good things to do for God. He wants to empower you to do His work because you were born to roar.

MY ROAR

Ask God to enlarge your imagination. Then ask Him to give you big ideas that can help bring His kingdom to earth. Record what He tells you in the *Pondering Paws* journal.

PONDERING PAWS

Ask God what He wants to say to you today about courage.
Pray for boldness and courage to do something great for God.

HELPING OUT

CHEW ON THIS
Our God gives you everything you need, makes you everything you're to be. 2 *Thessalonians* 1:2 (MSG)

UNDER THE TREE

While walking through the African bush, a lion encountered a horde of 20 hyenas. They were menacing, just like the hyenas in the movie *The Lion King*. The fearless lion could take on one or two hyenas and win easily, but being surrounded by 20 would be unnerving even for a powerful lion. It's bullying to the nth degree. Fortunately, the lion's cry for help alerted his cousin who immediately appeared. These two brave lions were able to scare off this bullying band of hyenas. Then they quietly strolled off together into the jungle.[23]

There are kids bullied every day in school, at sports events, and more. Maybe you can be like the cousin lion and help. Fifteen-year-old Trisha is like that cousin lion in the story. She saw kids being bullied online and appeared on the scene. She had heard of an 11-year-old girl who took her own life due to cyber bullying. It touched her deeply and made her angry. Trisha may not have known that she was tapping into God's heart, but she was.

God hates bullying and any kind of abuse. Trisha knew something had to be done. She wondered, "What would make kids aware of the pain caused by bullying?" Trisha came up with ReThink™, a software invention that stops hateful words online. Her software spots hateful, mean phrases that may be used against someone. It's genius! The user is then asked to stop and think before posting. She has pop-up windows that comment on bullying and the hateful speech.

God can give us an idea that changes the hearts of girls and guys. With ReThink™, kids have changed their mind 93% of the time and decided not to post a mean, hateful, abusive message.[24] God can use you to change the world because you were born to roar.

MY ROAR

Can you help someone who is being bullied? Pray for them and tell an adult your concerns. If you can, talk to the person being bullied and encourage them to get help. Ask God for some words for them that build up and cheer up.

PONDERING PAWS

Read about the dreamer Joseph who was bullied by his brothers.
Read Genesis 37:1–36 to find out what happened to him.
Journal about how your dreams and passions are progressing.

THE JESUS CHAIR (PART 1)

CHEW ON THIS

The LORD is with you when you are with him. If you seek him, he will be found by you. 2 *Chronicles* 15:2 (NIV)

UNDER THE TREE

Do you trust Jesus to be with you? One school day, 21 orphan children in South America put down their pencils. The orphans were having trouble focusing on their school work, so their teacher told them to forget about their homework for the day. "Let's lift our eyes toward heaven and invite Jesus to come," she said. The Holy Spirit came and started powerfully moving upon the kids' hearts. Two girls, Nissi (6) and Junery (7), took inviting Jesus into the room literally. They got an actual chair for Him and sat it in the center of them all.

Junery decided she wanted to crawl up in the Jesus chair and sit on Jesus' lap. As she sat in the chair, she began to feel safe and warm. It felt like someone had wrapped a blanket around her. Suddenly, a soft, sweet voice began whispering into her ear. Jesus was speaking to her. In a loving tone, He spoke promises to her about her family, but the words that pierced her heart the most were, "You're a princess, Junery."

Jesus knew everything about her. He knew her family couldn't care for her, so the whispers brought hope to her heart that she'd have parents one day. It was Jesus loving on her. She sat still, listening attentively. Overcome with tears, she jumped down and fell into the arms of her teacher. The teacher held her and sang worship songs to Jesus.

Then, Nissi and Junery decided they wanted to sing something special for Jesus. They knelt at the chair and began to sing "Perfume a Tus Pies," a Spanish worship song that means "Perfume at Your Feet."[25]

This true story tells us that Jesus loves us and wants to make His presence known to us. Jesus saw the children's needs and their desire for Him, so He was actually willing to sit in the Jesus chair. There is a Jesus chair for you—a place close to His heart. You don't have to wait to be an adult to know Jesus and sense His presence. Draw close to Him, and He will draw close to you. That's because you were born to roar.

MY ROAR

Go into your bedroom or pick a quiet place and invite Jesus to come in. If you want to, put a chair in the center of your room. Invite Jesus to come and sit with you.

PONDERING PAWS

Journal your own Jesus chair experience.
What is Jesus saying to you?

THE JESUS CHAIR (PART 2)

UNDER THE TREE

The Jesus chair story did not end that first day. The two girls, Nissi and Junery, went to school the next morning. The children had a visitor come to their school room. It was the cousin of one of the women who helped to care for them. She was in pain and suffered from swollen legs due to bad veins. The cousin went into the classroom and grabbed the first chair she saw. Guess what chair she sat in? Yes! It was the Jesus chair.

The woman immediately felt peace when she sat down in the Jesus chair. Then she noticed something strange. No more pain! Shocked, she stood up and began testing her legs. She noticed there was a paper taped to the back of the chair. Looking closer, she read, "Aqui se sienta Jesus" or "Here sits Jesus."

Filled with joy, she kicked her legs into the air and danced around the room. Her heart was happy, and she shouted praise to Jesus. She thanked Him over and over for healing her. The next day she felt giddy and light. It was the first morning in a long time she woke up without pain. She went to her job in peace without aching legs.[26]

This is such a great example of the childlike faith that the Bible speaks about. The children in the school had simply invited Jesus in. He loves to show up, speak to His children, and heal them. He is such a good Father. You, too, can make a difference in the lives of the others. You were born to roar!

MY ROAR

Make a sign that says "Here sits Jesus" and tape it to something in your room. Let it remind you that Jesus is always near.

PONDERING PAWS

Write a letter to Jesus, telling Him how much you love Him.
Wait and let Him respond, and record what you hear Him say.

A Good Father

CHEW ON THIS
LORD my God, I called to you for help, and you healed me.
Psalm 30:2 (NIV)

UNDER THE TREE

Little Henry hadn't stood or walked since he was born. He cried out in pain every time he tried to support his own weight. His knees were twisted, and his legs were weak from a lack of play. The neighborhood kids cared about his condition. These kids were as bold as lions. They believed that Jesus is the same yesterday, today, and forever. When they learned the Lord's Prayer in Sunday school, it stirred them up inside. Their favorite part of the prayer was when Jesus said, *Your kingdom come, your will be done, on earth as it is in heaven* (Matthew 6:10, NIV). Thoughts from the prayer turned their hearts toward heaven. In heaven, there is no pain when you try to walk. There is no sickness or hurt feelings in heaven. If we believe the Lord's Prayer, then Henry shouldn't have pain when he tries to walk, right?

The kids felt compassion for their little friend, so they decided to gather around Henry and pray for him. With their authority purchased by the cross of Jesus, they told the pain to leave. They said a simple prayer and asked their Papa God to heal Henry. Henry sat still on the ground, holding his stuffed bear while they prayed. After they prayed, Henry didn't just walk again—he immediately started running! He ran and ran and ran until he couldn't run anymore.[27]

We can thank God that He's our healer and that He loves His children. Heaven can touch earth when we believe God's Word. Heaven can touch earth when children are bold enough to pray. You'll see His kingdom come on earth as in heaven when you step into your roar.

MY ROAR

Is there someone you know who needs
a healing touch from heaven?
Be bold and ask them if you can pray for them.
Step out and pray, believing that God can heal.

PONDERING PAWS

See how many verses in the New Testament you can find on healing.

TURN AROUND PRAYERS

CHEW ON THIS

Is anyone among you in trouble? Let them pray. Is anyone happy?
Let them sing songs of praise. Is anyone among you sick? Let them call
the elders of the church to pray over them and anoint them with oil in
the name of the Lord. *James* 5:13–14 (NIV)

UNDER THE TREE

An eight-year-old boy nicknamed R2 weighed one pound five ounces at birth. At 24 weeks, his father's wedding ring fit around R2's tiny wrist. He was called a preemie. That's because he was born prematurely. His little body wasn't fully developed at the time of his birth. R2 had many physical problems as he began to grow. By the age of eight, he began to lose the ability to talk and walk. He loved singing and dancing and even that stopped. One day, his parents took him to the hospital. The doctors ran tests and found a dangerous brain condition. He was not expected to recover. Poor R2 lay in a fetal position for 3 months as his condition got worse and worse.

Eleven year-old Dori loved going to the prayer house with her parents. She had learned how to bring her worship into her prayers. So one day during worship, a movie picture came into her mind. She saw a room full of children praying. Their prayers began falling into a big golden bowl held by Jesus. The dream meant that God was telling her to collect friends to pray and worship together.

Then, when she heard about R2's condition, she sprang into action. Dori and her friends began praying for a turn around in R2's body. They made cards and pictures and gave them to R2's father. One of the pictures showed R2 sitting under a tree. Another one showed him singing and dancing.

One day, R2 woke up and began eating. and he ate all day. He began walking and talking again. He even went back to school. The children's prayers for a turn around were answered by Father God.[28] Your prayers are effective and powerful. You can change the world through prayer because you were born to roar.

MY ROAR

Gather some friends from church or school and create your own prayer team. Ask your parents for a recipe box and index cards. Begin writing the names of people, places, and things you are praying about. Somehow mark the cards as God answers prayer. Here are some categories you can pray about:

Families (fathers and mothers) • *School*
Friends • *City* • *Your Nation*

PONDERING PAWS

Sit with your journal and listen to your favorite worship music.
Write down or draw a picture of what you hear God saying to you.

_____

_____

_____

_____

_____

_____

_____

_____

_____

_____

_____

_____

_____

_____

_____

_____

_____

_____

_____

BE A FUNNEL

UNDER THE TREE

You have a huge roar! Picture your mouth opening up and a sound coming out that goes far and wide. Your roar can be an action or something you say. God uses kids to speak forth His words. God can take your voice and say amazing things through you.

Twelve-year-old Natasha became God's mouthpiece one Sunday morning at her church. With no fear and a lioness roar, she taught God's Word to 4,000 adults. Her message was called, "Be a Funnel." If this young girl can speak a message from God, you can too. Let her words encourage you to write your own message. You were born to roar like her.

NATASHA'S MESSAGE:

"How many of you know what an umbrella does? It keeps the rain from touching you. How many of you know what a funnel does? It receives the rain. Rain is God's blessings. 1 Kings 18:41 says, "There is a sound of abundance of rain." You see, the rain won't stop until you receive it. You have to receive God's blessings and His presence.

"I was at the pool with my next-door neighbor and friend. I was praying for my friend who was having a hard time. I had my funnel up and open, and I was receiving a lot of water. So, when I prayed for my friend, he received Jesus as His Savior.

"John 3:30 says you decrease so He can increase. Many of you may want to be a funnel. But, if you don't have your funnel up and open, you can't pray His way. Stand up and hold your hand up like a funnel, and let God rain upon you. God, rain and pour on us, pour on us. The blessings come in when your funnel opens. Some of you need something in your life and in your heart. He is the King of kings and Lord of lords. It doesn't matter what your neighbor thinks of you, but what God thinks of you."[29]

What a great word from God. It is so simple, yet so lion-like. You can do it too because you were born to roar.

MY ROAR

Try writing your own message from God. Ask your Sunday school teacher if you can share it with your class. Or, present it to your family or friends. Here are some things you might put into your message:

A scripture • A life lesson • One or two examples
Something in nature or something we use daily

PONDERING PAWS

Select a favorite scripture from your Bible. Ask God to explain its meaning
or meanings to you. Write down what you hear.

What's on a LION'S MENU

Antelope – Reading your Bible and praying every day will help you grow and hear God's voice.

Birds – Let God love you. Open your heart to Him every day.

Bison – Allow God to roar through your speech and actions and become a world changer.

Buffalo – Forgive fast and often!

Elephant – Listen for God's voice, expecting Him to speak to you in a variety of ways.

Gazelle – Talk to God and think of Him daily.

Giraffe – Make Jesus your best friend.

Hippo – Live creatively and use your gifts for God; you can invent something. Listen for God-ideas to come to you.

Lizard – Think of ways to help and serve others daily or weekly.

Mice – Freely share your feelings with God and others.

Rabbit – Heal the sick.

Rhino – Encourage and love others.

Wild Hog – Be a son or daughter of God.

Wildebeest – Be yourself and walk free from fear.

Zebra – Never give up!

Develop a lion-like appetite that can strengthen you to change the world!

ROARING THROUGH THE WORD

DAILY BIBLE READING (70 DAYS)

Want to read secret highlights from every Book of the Bible? It doesn't take long! After you finish this devotional book, set up a Bible reading plan. As you read, ask Jesus to help you understand and personalize His words. Thank God for what He's doing in each area of your life. Respond to God and journal through each question about the scripture. Remember, picture journaling is just as fun as writing things down.

DAY 1   GENESIS 1 AND 2
Question: God, why did You create people and especially me?

DAY 2   GENESIS 28
Question: God, what would You like to show me about heaven?

DAY 3   EXODUS 3
Question: God, what do You want to say to me when I stop what I'm doing to focus on You?

DAY 4   EXODUS 20
Question: God, which of the Ten Commandments do You want me to work on right now?

DAY 5   NUMBERS 21 AND 27
Question: God, what do I need to receive courage for in my life? Help me, Lord!

DAY 6   DEUTERONOMY 6
Question: God, what do I put before You in my life?

DAY 7   DEUTERONOMY 28
Question: God, where in my life do I need to obey Your voice?

DAY 8   JOSHUA 1 AND 6
Question: God, where do You want to make Yourself known in my city? I'm praying You will take control of that land.

DAY 9   JUDGES 5 AND 6
Question: Gideon was the weakest among his tribe, but God called him a man of valor. God, what do You call me when I am weak?

DAY 10   RUTH 4
Question: God, help me write a prayer about always following You.

DAY 11   1 SAMUEL 2 AND 3
Question: God, where do You want me to meet with You each day?

DAY 12   2 SAMUEL 6 AND 7
Question: Focus on 7:8–13. God, what kind of a leader do You want me to be? Where do You want me to lead others?

DAY 13   1 KINGS 17
Question: God, in what area of my life do I need to trust You?

*Scriptures using the word "roar"

DAY 14 1 KINGS 18:20—19:10 *(18:41)
Question: Is there anyone bullying you?
Journal about it and tell an adult about it.

DAY 15 2 KINGS 2 AND 6
Question: Have you lost a friend or
parent? God, I miss _____ so much.
Here is what I loved about them....

DAY 16 1 CHRONICLES 7 AND 12
Question: God, why are families so
important to You?

DAY 17 1 CHRONICLES 20 AND 25
Question: God, what or who are the
Goliaths, or giants, in my life? How do You
want me to defeat them?

DAY 18 2 CHRONICLES 7 AND 29
Question: God, tell me something I need
to pray about today.

DAY 19 EZRA 3
Question: God, what kind and type of
offering can I give You today?

DAY 20 NEHEMIAH 1—3
Question: God, is there an important
job, situation, person, place, project, or
anything I need to help rebuild?

DAY 21 NEHEMIAH 4 AND 6
Question: Focus on 4:18. God, what do I
have beside me to help fight the battles of
the enemy (devil)?

DAY 22 ESTHER 1 AND 2
Question: God, how are You preparing me
for something great?

DAY 23 ESTHER 3—5
Question: God, what should I do when I
am afraid to take a risk for You?

DAY 24 ESTHER 6—8
Question: Focus on 8:2. God, what does
Your signet ring look like? (Draw what you
think He shows you).

DAY 25 JOB 33:14–17
Question: Does God speak to you in your
dreams? Ask God for the meaning of one
of your dreams. Write out your dream and
God's response to it.

DAY 26 PSALMS 1 AND 23
* (38:8, 42:7, 46:3, 46:6)
Question: Focus on 23:5. God, what would
be on a table that You set in front of me?

DAY 27 PSALMS 51 AND 100
* (65:7, 74:4, 83:2, 93:4)
Question: Focus on Psalm 100. Write a
song to Father God, and sing it to Him.

DAY 28 PSALM 139
* (96:11, 98:7, 104:21)
Question: God, tell me what Your thoughts
are toward me.

DAY 29 PROVERBS 2 AND 21 * (20:2)
Question: God, give me a secret word of
wisdom about something I am afraid of.
(Wisdom is the right words or actions at
the right time.)

DAY 30 ECCLESIASTES 5
Question: Journal what season your heart
feels right now: spring (learning new
things), summer (happy and content), fall
(ready for change), or winter (life is sad or
hard right now).

DAY 31 SONG OF SOLOMON 1 AND 8
Question: God, do You love me? Tell me
why You love me.

DAY 32 ISAIAH 6 AND 11
* (5:29–30, 13:4, 17:12–13, 51:15, 59:11)
Question: Focus on 6:1. God, what is Your
favorite victory in the Bible? Journal about
a victory in your life. (Note: The length of
the train of a king's robe represents his
victories over the enemy. The longer the
robe, the more wins!)

DAY 33 ISAIAH 55 AND 61
Question: God, if it cost Jesus everything
to give me life, what should it cost me to
live for Him?

**DAY 34 JEREMIAH 1 AND 2;
LAMENTATIONS 3** * (All Jeremiah 2:15, 4:13,
5:22, 6:23, 11:16, 10:22, 25:30, 31:35, 50:42,
51:16)
Question: Focus on Jeremiah 1:11–13.
What do you see? God, teach me to
see what You see. Let God use your
imagination to show you a picture.
Journal what you see!

DAY 35   EZEKIEL 1—3, 37 * (1:24, 43:2)
Question: God, what do You look like? Do I look like You in any way?

DAY 36   DANIEL 1—2, 4—6
Question: Focus on 1:8. God, give me ideas! How do I keep myself from following friends when they want to do wrong?

DAY 37   HOSEA 6 AND JOEL 2
* (Hosea 11:10)
Question: God, name one way I can love You more than the world. Also, if You pour out Your Spirit on all flesh, does that include kids?

DAY 38   AMOS 3 AND OBADIAH
* (Amos 1:2, 3:4)
Question: God, tell me one of Your secrets about how to _____.

DAY 39   JONAH
Question: God, why did You send Jonah into a whale for three days? What should I learn from Jonah's experience?

DAY 40   HABAKKUK 2 AND ZEPHANIAH 2
Question: God, tell me where I am being patient and waiting well. Help me where I am not.

DAY 41   HAGGAI 2
Question: God, what kind of a message do You want me to share with my friends and family?

DAY 42   ZECHARIAH 4 AND MALACHI 4 * (Zechariah 9:15)
Question: God, give me ideas on how I can love and honor one or both of my parents.

DAY 43   MATTHEW 1—3
Question: God told Jesus He was a good Son. He wants to tell you why you are a good son or daughter. What is God saying to you?

DAY 44   MATTHEW 5 AND 21
Question: Jesus, which of the Beatitudes is Your favorite from Matthew 5:1–12? Why do You like it?

DAY 45   MATTHEW 25 AND 28
Question: How well do You know me, God? What do You like about me? Here is what I like about You! _____.

DAY 46   MARK 4 AND 7
Question: God, where does fear come from? What's the opposite of fear? Here are the things I am afraid of: _____. Help me with fear, Lord.

DAY 47   LUKE 1 AND 2
Question: God, what are Your promises for me as a son or daughter?

DAY 48   LUKE 10 AND 11
Question: Write out the Lord's Prayer from Luke 11. Ask God to explain any part you don't understand.

DAY 49   LUKE 15 AND 17 * (21:25)
Question: God, show me anyone I need to forgive for hurting me. Lead me in a prayer of forgiveness. Help me erase the hurt from my heart.

DAY 50   JOHN 1 AND 5
Question: God, here is a list of friends and family members who need Your healing. Help me write healing prayers for them.

DAY 51   JOHN 10 AND 17
Question: God, I hear You, and You hear me. As I tell You my feelings, can You tell me Yours?

DAY 52   ACTS 2 AND 9 * (2:2, 22:22)
Question: God, what is the Holy Spirit like? Tell me some things You want me to know about Him.

DAY 53   ACTS 10 AND 11
Question: Focus on 10:34–35. God, who do I need to reach out to and include in friendship? Is there anyone I have treated mean because they are different? What should I do about it?

DAY 54   ROMANS 6 AND 8
Question: God, am I feeling shame in any area where You have forgiven me? Am I hanging on to something You have set me free from?

DAY 55   ROMANS 12 AND 15
Question: God, what thoughts do You want to put in my mind about You?

DAY 56   1 CORINTHIANS 12—14
Question: God, what spiritual gift do You want to give me? Also, who do I need to love more?

DAY 57   2 CORINTHIANS 3 AND 4
Question: God, what do You mean when You say, *The Spirit gives life* (2 Corinthians 3:6, NIV)? What do You want to say to me today about the Holy Spirit in my life?

DAY 58   GALATIANS 5 AND 6
Question: God, show me a heart or mind picture of You and me hanging out, doing something fun.

DAY 59   EPHESIANS 1, 4 AND 6
Question: God, how do You want Jesus to lead me? In other words, how do You want me to follow Jesus?

DAY 60   PHILIPPIANS 2 AND 4
Question: God, the Bible says I can do all things through Christ. Here is what I want to do, God….

DAY 61   COLOSSIANS 1 AND 3
Question: Focus on 3:2. God, as I sit with You, turn my mind toward things in heaven. Now, God, what do You want me to see?

DAY 62   1 THESSALONIANS 4 AND 2 THESSALONIANS 3
Question: God, help me write a promise to You to keep my eyes from looking at unclean images.

DAY 63   1 TIMOTHY 1 AND 4
Question: God, what gifts and talents have You given to me? How do You want me to use them at school, home, church, sports, dance, and more?

DAY 64   2 TIMOTHY 1 AND 2
Question: God, why do people in our lives hurt us? I'll bet You know who has hurt me. Help me to write a note to You about forgiving them for how they hurt me.

DAY 65   TITUS 3 AND PHILEMON
Question: God, what do You want to teach me from my reading today?

DAY 66   HEBREWS 3, 5, AND 11
Question: Focus on 11. Faith is believing God even though you can't see Him. Many people in the Bible were filled with faith through every trial. Ask: God, who was most faithful to You in the Bible? Write down everything God has done for you.

DAY 67 JAMES 1 AND 3
Question: God, where am I pleasing You? Where in my life do I need to please You more?

DAY 68   1 PETER 5 AND 2 PETER 1
* (2 Peter 3:10)
Question: Humility is thinking of yourself less often. Ask: God, show me where I need to think of myself less often? Then ask Him where you need to think of yourself more.

DAY 69   1 JOHN 3, 2 JOHN, AND 3 JOHN
Question: God, how do You need me to love You in more ways and more often?

DAY 70   JUDE AND REVELATION 4, 19:6—21: 22 * (Rev. 1:15, 9:9, 10:3, 14:2, 19:6)
Question: God, mark me for Your work on the earth. God, if You put Your own brand upon my arm, what would the picture on the brand look like?

END NOTES

1 "5 Amazing Kids Who Make a Difference." Habitat for Humanity. Accessed April 02, 2019. https://www.habitat.org/stories/5-amazing-kids-who-make-a-difference.

2 "14 Awesome Stories of Exceptionally Brave Children." Storypick. February 02, 2016. Accessed April 02, 2019. https://www.storypick.com/child-bravery/.

3 Breyer, Melissa. "6 Incredible Treasures Found with a Metal Detector." MNN. June 05, 2017. Accessed April 02, 2019. https://www.mnn.com/earth-matters/wilderness-resources/stories/6-incredible-treasures-found-with-a-metal-detector.

4 "Claws Protract to Grip Prey: Lion." AskNature. Accessed April 03, 2019. https://asknature.org/strategy/claws-protract-to-grip-prey/#.XKT7gi2ZMk8.

5 "Harnessed Lions" story based on: "I SAW THE KING'S CARRIAGE." The Harness of the Lord, by Bill Britton. Accessed April 03, 2019. http://www.promiseed.com/articles/fathers/b_britton/harness.html.

6 "David's Sling and Stones: Were They Toys or Serious Weapons?" • KidExplorers • ChristianAnswers.Net. Accessed April 03, 2019. https://christiananswers.net/q-abr/abr-slingsforkids.html.

7 "Lion Anatomy: The Eye." Safari Guide Online. April 06, 2014. Accessed April 03, 2019. https://danielpeel.wordpress.com/2011/10/03/lion-anatomy-the-eye/.

8 "Divine Intervention: Lions Save Christians from Islamic Militants!" God TV. October 29, 2018. Accessed April 03, 2019. https://godtv.com/miracle-lions/.

9 Story adapted from Aesop's Fable Collection

10 Knapton, Sarah. "African Elephants Have the Best Smell in the Animal Kingdom." The Telegraph. July 23, 2014. Accessed April 04, 2019. https://www.telegraph.co.uk/news/earth/wildlife/10984345/African-elephants-have-the-best-smell-in-the-animal-kingdom.html.

11 Nargi, Lela. "Taste Good? Senses Inform the Brain, but Don't Tell Everyone the Same Thing." Science News for Students. August 02, 2018. Accessed April 04, 2019. https://www.sciencenewsforstudents.org/article/taste-good-senses-inform-brain-dont-tell-everyone-same-thing.

12 Wood, Larry. "Colors of Salvation." Colors in Scripture. Accessed April 04, 2019. http://www.biblenews1.com/colors/colors.html.

13-14 Johnson, Beni. The Happy Intercessor. Shippensburg, PA: Destiny Image Pubishers, 2009.

15 "Frank Epperson Invents the Popsicle, 1905." Inventive Kids. June 28, 2016. Accessed April 05, 2019. http://inventivekids.com/frank-epperson-invents-the-popsicle/.

16 "Chester Greenwood Biography, List of Chester Greenwood Inventions." Edubilla.com. Accessed April 05, 2019. http://www.edubilla.com/inventor/chester-greenwood/.

17 "Symbols of Christmas: The Story of Christmas Lights." SayWhyDoI.com. Accessed April 05, 2019. http://www.saywhydoi.com/symbols-of-christmas-the-story-of-christmas-lights/.

18 Ament, Phil. Christmas Tree Lights History - Invention of Christmas Tree Lights. January 01, 1970. Accessed April 05, 2019. http://www.ideafinder.com/history/inventions/christlights.html.

19 Astill, James. "Lioness Adopts Another Antelope." The Guardian. February 17, 2002. Accessed April 05, 2019. https://www.theguardian.com/world/2002/feb/17/jamesastill.theobserver.

20 McGlensey, Melissa. "This 9-Year-Old Built a Nonprofit, No-Kill Animal Shelter Out of His Garage to Help Stray Animals." HuffPost. December 07, 2017. Accessed April 05, 2019. https://www.huffpost.com/entry/happy-animals-club_n_5324863.

21 Shandrow, Kim Lachance. "11 Successful Kid Entrepreneurs Keeping Their Eyes on the Prize." Entrepreneur. August 04, 2016. Accessed April 05, 2019. https://www.entrepreneur.com/slideshow/273222#11.

22 Utley, Tori. "13-Year-Old Founder Mercer Henderson Is Creating Apps to Make a Difference." Forbes. October 31, 2016. Accessed April 05, 2019. https://www.forbes.com/sites/toriutley/2016/10/31/13-year-old-founder-mercer-henderson-is-creating-apps-to-make-a-difference/#401c252a2c9c.

23 Person. "Lion Attacked by Pack of Hyenas." BBC Earth. November 23, 2018. Accessed April 05, 2019. https://www.bbcearth.com/blog/?article=lion-attacked-by-pack-of-hyenas.

24 Harris, Jo. "This 15-year-old's Anti-cyber-bullying Invention Is AWESOME." Kidspot. July 03, 2017. Accessed April 05, 2019. https://www.kidspot.com.au/parenting/real-life/in-the-news/this-15yearolds-anticyberbullying-invention-is-awesome/news-story/7a4bd0d13778b10e51fb117b8cf71a39.

25-27 Story as told to me by missionary Kara Westermann. December 18, 2018, Iris Global Beauty for Ashes – Managua, Nicaragua. https://www.irisglobal.org/nicaragua

28 Worship, Richy Clark // Radiant. "The Power of Praying Children - R2 Testimony - Richy Clark." YouTube. April 10, 2013. Accessed April 05, 2019. https://www.youtube.com/watch?v=OQ_g3gL-3cs.

29 Howard-Browne, Rodney. "Be a Funnel." YouTube. July 08, 2016. Accessed April 05, 2019. https://www.youtube.com/watch?v=VtS_tVCyHIs.

ABOUT THE AUTHOR

Diane Cory carries a message that imparts a lifestyle of encouragement that comes through intimacy with God.

She has a bachelor's degree in elementary education and a master's and endorsement in early childhood education. She is the author of the bestselling children's devotionals *Gotta Have God* for boys and *God & Me* for girls. She has also been a contributing writer for mainline Sunday school curriculum.

In 2007, along with her husband Scott and their sons, she founded Extreme Youth Community. EYC operated for six years as a non-profit, equipping school for children ages 8-12, training children in ministry and giving them the opportunity to know the Holy Spirit. Her passion to see children in ministry led to a short season of hosting a radio program called "Children in Ministry Today."

She is a wife and mother of three grown sons, along with two daughters-in-law and four grandchildren. She makes her home in Omaha, Nebraska.

A NOTE FROM THE AUTHOR

My passion is to cultivate personal intimacy with God: loving His presence, hearing His voice, and teaching others to hear Him—whether they are children or adults. My prayer is that this book will stir all who read it to understand God's heart for children and His desire to see them find their purpose in Him now.

If you have enjoyed this book, please let me know. You can contact me at **dlcory1@hotmail.com.**